SECRETS
OF THE BLESSED

SECRETS
OF THE BLESSED

QUIET MEDITATIONS FOR TROUBLED HEARTS

CHARLES A. LEMASTER

GSH

ISBN: 978-1-956074-48-2 (Paperback Edition)
ISBN: 978-1-956074-49-9 (Hardcover Edition)
ISBN: 978-1-956074-47-5 (E-book Edition)

Book Ordering Information

Phone Number: 315 288-7939 ext. 1000 or 347-901-4920
Email: info@globalsummithouse.com
Global Summit House
www.globalsummithouse.com

Printed in the United State of America

To My Three Sons

Chuck, Chad and Chet

I'm often asked how long it took me to write this book. My answer is always the same: "Not very long, but it took me forty years to learn the lessons. You have live with me through those years and yet, you still love me.

ACKNOWLEDGMENTS

So many people through the years have given immeasurable contribution to this work by simply listening, reflection and sharing with me what they have learned through their relationship with Christ. I think first of my pastors at Parkview Church: David Ziegle, Brad Martin, and Steve Rudisill. Thank you, gentlemen, for seeing in me someone you could encourage in the ministry for Christ.

I am thankful for friends like Dan Little and Jim Pauley who invested their lives teaching their pastor how to fish and hunt while we so often discussed the scriptures. You probably are unaware of the impact you had on my thinking.

Some big special thanks go out to the "Hope" Sunday school class I am privileged to lead. You dear folks keep me balanced and you've challenged me so many times to think more carefully when I am apt to generalize.

I am so appreciative of my wife, Pam, for her support, encouragement, and love through this project. You've kept a close eye on my moods and have insisted that I "step away from the computer" when you have watched me stressing out. Thank you, Honey! Thank you for believing in me.

No work like this can be done without those willing to proof read and offer insights. It is so easy to read words I only imagine I have included in the narrative. Some special thanks go to my brother, Doug Lemaster for your critical thinking that certainly helped my clarity of thought, to my sister Claudette Presley for proof reading the manuscript and to Halley Moore for your copy editing.

Dad, you have given me so much encouragement to get this book in print, I think I can hear your applause from heaven.

TABLE OF CONTENTS

WELCOME TO SECRETS OF THE BLESSED

No one ever promised life had to be fair but does it have to hurt so much? Is there any hope that this pain will ever end?

Wherever Jesus went he was surrounded by a multitude of hurting people, folks that needed someone to care about and for them. He saw them as harassed, scattered sheep in desperate need of a shepherd. To each of us he has brought hope for deliverance, healing from our sorrows and forgiveness for our sins.

Whether we investigate the heartbeat of the Psalmists, the trials of the patriarchs or the pains of the apostles, we find people who faced the abuse life arbitrarily hurls our way. These saints found healing through their relationship with their God. They wrote fearlessly of their experiences so we might learn from them.

Secrets of the Blessed takes us on a journey of faith through our pain. There is hope for a blessed, happy life when we learn to believe God, even when he seems unfair to us. There one secret I missed for most of my life. In it is a gold mine of truth we can never exhaust. It is found in Ephesians 1:3, "Blessed be the God and Father of our Lord Jesus Christ, who has blessed us with every spiritual blessing in the heavenly places in Christ," (NASB). This is the key secret: we have already been blessed with all his spiritual blessings! It now up to us to appropriate them.

As a former pastor, it is hard to admit I had to learn most of life's lessons the hard way, but such is the nature of the ministry. It seemed to me that my job as a preacher was twofold: to afflict the comfortable and to comfort the afflicted. Sadly, I spent far too much energy trying to do the impossible task afflicting the comfortable.

About midway through my years as a pastor, I realized (finally) that most folks in my congregations were believers in Christ who were struggling in their spiritual lives as much as I was in mine. These dear fellow pilgrims did not need me to tell them how bad they were because they were already painfully aware of their faults. They desperately needed someone to show them a better way and lead them to a happier life.

Since that time, it has been the desire of my heart to give hope to hurting people. These studies are called the "Secrets of the Blessed" (or Happy), with a burning desire in my heart to be, as another has stated, "one beggar showing other beggars where to find bread."

When we are going through the painful events of our lives, it seems the universe must hold some hidden agenda depriving us of joy and peace. Instead of surrendering to such darkness, I invite you to join with me on this pilgrimage of faith through our pain. As we take each step, let's search the Scriptures together to find hope for our hurting hearts.

PART 1

FINDING FAITH IN OUR FALLEN WORLD

CHAPTER 1

DOES JESUS CARE? I MEAN DOES HE CARE FOR ME?

Jesus cares about people. Nowhere is that fact more evident than it is in the Gospels. During the years of his ministry, he walked from town to town, village to village, and even city to city. Great crowds of people would gather to hear him preach and to feel the touch of his healing hands.

He was so busy at times, his mother and brothers thought he was losing his mind from all the stress, and they sought to rescue him. He was so tired he fell asleep in the bow of a boat during a storm that frightened seasoned fishermen. He was always with people, and even taking little children up in his arms to bless them. He was pressed on every side, but still he recognized when a needy woman touched just the hem of his clothes.

People, people, everywhere, but he never complained. Thousands gathered on the hillsides to listen to him teach for three days. When it was time to end this marathon seminar, they were so hungry they were in danger of fainting. So, much to his disciples' surprise, he fed them all from the scant resources they found--a little boy's lunch.

He healed the sick. He cast out demons. The blind could see. The deaf could hear. The lame walked. The mute talked. Why, he even raised the dead. All this happened because Jesus cared about people.

Matthew recorded Jesus's response to all these people. "Jesus went through all the towns and villages, teaching in their synagogues, proclaiming the good news of the kingdom and healing every disease and sickness. When he saw the crowds, he had compassion on them, because they were harassed and helpless, like sheep without a shepherd" (Matthew 9:35–36 NIV).

Jesus was moved with *compassion*. That means Jesus felt something inside. It is all one word, which means, literally, "the bowels." When we talk about our emotions, we talk about how our heart feels. In the first century, the seat of human emotion was the general area of organs.

I think we can identify with the concept. I have often felt that sinking, hurting, sickening feeling in my chest and the pit of my stomach when seeing or hearing of the calamity of someone I love. Sometimes it happens when watching the news and hear of the abuse that has been heaped on the innocent.

When Jesus saw this great crowd of people, he was moved internally. He felt compassion for these people. Why? It was not just because they had physical needs. He had been taking care of those. What moved him was a threefold observation: They were harassed, helpless, and aimless—like sheep without a shepherd.

Jesus looked beyond the obvious to see what was going on in their innermost being. Matthew recalled the words of the prophet Isaiah as he reflected on Jesus's healing ministry: "A bruised reed he will not break, and a smoldering wick he will not snuff out" (Matthew 12:20 NIV). We may be bruised, but he will not break us. We may be smoldering like a lamp that is out of oil, but he won't quench us. He heals bruises and ignites glowing embers.

"The Spirit of the Lord is on me, because he has anointed me to proclaim good news to the poor. He has sent me to proclaim freedom for the prisoners and recovery of sight for the blind, to set the oppressed free, to proclaim the year of the Lord's favor" (Luke 4:18–19 NIV).

He came to share the good news with us. It is the news of eternal life through his finished work on the cross and resurrection. We have been slaves of sin, but his blood frees us. We were born spiritually blind, but now we see. This was his mission.

He cares for us. It is not just the love that compelled him to the cross. It is his compassion for us, his hurting bride. The ache in his heart for us sent him to bring deliverance from our harassers, hope in our helplessness, and guidance in our aimlessness.

"Come to me, all you who are weary and burdened, and I will give you rest. Take my yoke upon you and learn from me, for I am gentle and humble in heart, and you will find rest for your souls. For my yoke is easy and my burden is light" (Matthew 11:28–30 NIV).

DOES JESUS CARE?
BY FRANK E. GRAEFF

PUBLIC DOMAINE

Does Jesus care when my heart is pained
Too deeply for mirth or song,
As the burdens press, and the cares distress,
And the way grows weary and long?

Refrain:
Oh, yes, He cares, I know He cares,
His heart is touched with my grief;
When the days are weary, the long nights dreary,
I know my Savior cares.

Does Jesus care when my way is dark
With a nameless dread and fear?
As the daylight fades into deep night shades,
Does He care enough to be near?

Does Jesus care when I've tried and failed
To resist some temptation strong;
When for my deep grief there is no relief,
Though my tears flow all the night long?

Does Jesus care when I've said "goodbye"
To the dearest on earth to me,
And my sad heart aches till it nearly breaks—
Is it aught to Him? Does He see?

CHAPTER 2

THERE'S AN APP FOR THAT!

At the risk of stating the obvious, there seems to be an over-abundance of apps for our smart phones for almost any- thing we might conceive. Some are extremely useful, others are convenient, and many are clever, cute, or entertaining.

Recently on the evening news, the reporter told of an app that is supposed to read the user's emotions by their facial expression. Maybe such a function could be useful because there are times when I don't really know what I feel. Probably more often than not, I do not know how to express what I feel. I guess that just goes along with being *male*.

On too many occasions, we might feel guilty or made to feel guilty about the emotions churning inside of us. Well-meaning friends tell us, "You shouldn't feel that way!" Truthfully, though, we *do* feel "that way," and as uncomfortable as the emotions may be, they are neither right nor wrong. They just are. For whatever reason, something hap- pens, and we respond internally.

The question then becomes, "Okay, I feel this way, and I don't like it! What do I do now?" Here's the answer. Are you ready?

There's an app for that!

Yes, you can download it to your phone or notepad. It's very user-friendly, and you might find yourself enthralled with it. It is apt to become your favorite app of all time. It is called the Bible App, or more specifically, the book of Psalms. I haven't counted them all, but so far, I have found comfort for every emotion I have experienced in that beautiful songbook.

Undoubtedly, the most valuable lesson I've learned is that it is okay for me to feel my emotions. God is not condemning me for them. Like the psalmist, I am free to fully express them to him. I can watch carefully as he skillfully weaves his plan into the writer's heart. Comfort floods my soul as I prepare to allow him to do the same for me.

The psalmist expresses the contradictions in himself as he repeatedly says, "Wait for the Lord; be strong and take heart and wait for the Lord" (Psalm 27:14 NIV), yet in a previous song, he cries, "How long, Lord? Will you forget me forever? How long will you hide your face from me?" (13:1 NIV).

Who hasn't felt this way at some dark times in their lives? It's good to know that David, the one known as the man after God's own heart, felt the sense of abandonment during troubled times in his life. He didn't stop with those few words. He continued pouring out his heart:

> How long must I wrestle with my thoughts and day after day have sorrow in my heart? How long will my enemy triumph over me? Look on me and answer, Lord my God. Give light to my eyes, or I will sleep in death, and my enemy will say, "I have overcome him," and my foes will rejoice when I fall. (verses 2–4 NIV)

His lament was long and sorrowful. But he had no fear of pouring his troubling thoughts out to his God. He knew that it was okay to tell God how he really felt about what was going on in his life. You know, we can do the same thing.

After all these expressions of grief and turmoil that came rolling off his lips, suddenly in verses 5–6, his attitude did an abrupt about-face: “But I trust in your unfailing love; my heart rejoices in your salvation. I will sing the Lord’s praise, for he has been good to me” (NIV).

David takes a step of faith. He remembers God loves him and God’s love never fails. Can a reversal in attitudes really happen that quickly, that easily? Not only does he trust, but he rejoices. Further still, he praises. He sings! And he realizes, he knows. He is not abandoned. He is not alone. I can see him singing with wide-open eyes, “He has been good to me.” Even during the times when he felt so alone, he discovered, “God is good all the time.”

CHAPTER 3

WHEN OUR FAITH FAILS US

Feeling my back was up against the wall with obsessive thoughts, studying Hebrews 11, the "Faith Hall of Fame" chapter, was not building my own faith. I thought it was mocking me. Depression was overwhelming, and the unshakable drive to just literally flee into the mountains was like an irresistible force compelling me forward to irrational behavior. Why couldn't I believe God enough to conquer my mind?

Don't get me wrong. There were what I call *faith events* in my life when believing God for deliverance did bring victory and peace into my life from these struggles. Those victories would sometimes last for days, maybe weeks, and once, for a year and a half. These days were marked by sweet peace and a freedom to walk with my Savior unmolested by depression or sinful compulsions.

But something always happened to end those wonderful days. It seemed like there were blitz attacks from hell against my soul. My faith failed me. I understood so little about what was going on. I was a pastor! I was a preacher of the Word and a teacher of the faith! Yet my faith was depleted.

For an extended time, I endured what I call the silence of heaven. I became desperate to hear from God, but heard only silence. Let me pause to just reassure us all that those times of quietness are part of God's design to draw us to himself. We wonder why our prayers go unanswered without realizing God is at work moving heaven and earth to make things happen in his time and his way.

Well, I'm not the only one to experience this faith crisis. The Jewish Christians in the book of Hebrews knew the up-and-down struggles of wavering faith:

> Remember those earlier days after you had received the light, when you endured in a great conflict full of suffering. Sometimes you were publicly exposed to insult and persecution; at other times you stood side by side with those who were so treated. You suffered along with those in prison and joyfully accepted the confiscation of your property, because you knew that you yourselves had better and lasting possessions. So do not throw away your confidence; it will be richly rewarded. (Hebrews 10:32–35 NIV)

These people knew the joy of victory in their walk with Christ even during terrible persecution. Times were hard, but their joy was full. My circumstances cannot begin to be compared with what these dear saints endured, but I can relate to their joy in a small way.

The problem was: the pressure did not let up. Earlier in chapter 10, and in chapter 6 as well as other places, these struggling believers were warned of the consequences of giving up. They were sorely tempted to go back to their old life of worship under the Jewish law of Moses. Apparently, there were some who had done just that.

Have you ever felt like throwing in the towel and giving up? Trust me, if you are truly God's child, God never gives up on you even if you try to give up on him. For me, giving up was the hardest thing I ever tried to do. Just as God moved the writer of Hebrews to encourage and warn these early believers, He continued to work away at my heart.

> You need to persevere so that when you have done the will of God, you will receive what he has promised. For, "In just a little while, he who is coming will come and will not delay." And, "But my righteous one will live by faith. And I take no pleasure in the one who shrinks back." But we do not belong to those who shrink back and are destroyed, but to those who have faith and are saved. (Hebrews 10:36–39 NIV)

These hurting people are offered hope. They are reminded of the promise of Christ's return. Their encouragement is the same as the one given in Habakkuk 2:4, and now for the third time in the New Testament, "My righteous one will live by faith" (see Romans 1:17, Galatians 3:11.

I believe the lesson here to be quite clear. Those who have a saving faith may go through terrific trials, but they do not give up. They do not shrink back. Yes, there have been difficult barren days. Desperate days in which our faith is tested do come. "These have come so that the proven genuineness of your faith—of greater worth than gold, which perishes even though refined by fire—may result in praise, glory and honor when Jesus Christ is revealed" (1 Peter 1:7 NIV).

So, when our faith appears to fail us, it is God's design to prove what our faith is really made of. Is it genuine? Yes? Then know this: you (I mean we can stand the test. Struggle? Yes. Fall? Maybe. Get back up? Certainly!

By the way, if your faith is under fire, you are struggling to make sense of it all, and you feel like you are imploding, take courage. This can be a good thing. It was for me.

CHAPTER 4

FAITH THAT NEVER FAILS

Words are important. Understanding what a word means is essential to processing any concept. As my wife and I watched preliminary analysis before our Bengals lost on Sunday to the Steelers, one of the talking heads (commentators) repeatedly used the word *acrimony*. I couldn't tell from the context what the word acrimony meant, so I asked Google and was informed means "animosity." Without that short definition, their conversation was making little sense to me.

I guess I've always been a simple sort of guy who needs language reduced to its most easily understood definitions. The word *faith* was one of those mystery words I did not understand, so I set out to discover its meaning reduced to the clearest terms possible. Since learning its meaning, I've spent a lifetime trying to comprehend its role in my spiritual life.

I guess what troubled me were thoughts like, "I guess I just don't have enough faith." "If I really had faith, I know my prayers would be answered." "My faith is so weak, I doubt my salvation all the time." These assumptions served as whipping posts in my walk with Christ. I was forever assaulted by guilt.

Understanding faith was complicated, only because I made it that way! The key lay in understanding the Bible's own definition of faith given in Hebrews 11:1, "Now faith is the assurance of things hoped for, the conviction of things not seen" (NASB).

The Greek word for *assurance* means, literally, "to stand under, a foundation, or underpinning." It is the picture of the massive beams and supports that hold a building up. Biblical hope is not the "Oh, I hope so!" wishful thinking type of hope. It carries instead the meaning of *certainty* and *expectation*. So "faith is the foundation of the things we expect."

Our hope is found in those things God has promised us. After telling us about our future resurrection and our glorified bodies, Paul calls it our *hope*. "For in hope we have been saved, but hope that is seen is not hope; for who hopes for what he already sees? But if we hope for what we do not see, with perseverance we wait eagerly for it" (Romans 8:24–25, NASB. Therefore, faith is the foundation for what God promised to us.

Faith is also the "conviction of things we do not see." He uses three illustrations to help us understand. First, in verse 3, "By faith we understand that the universe was formed at God's command, so that what is seen was not made out of what was visible" (NIV). In all of creation, here we have the only eyewitness account of how the universe came to be. God made it all out of nothing. How do I know? God said so. Therefore, I believe it. That is faith.

In the second illustration, Abel worshipped. "By faith, Abel brought God a better offering than Cain did. By faith he was commended as righteous, when God spoke well of his offerings. And by faith Abel still speaks, even though he is dead" (verse 4 NIV). I learned through the Scriptures that I cannot come to God through the works of my hands as Cain tried, but by the blood of the Lamb. That is faith.

In the third illustration, Enoch pleased God by faith. "By faith Enoch was taken from this life, so that he did not experience death: 'He could not be found, because God had taken him away.' For before he was taken, he was commended as one who pleased God" (verse 5 NIV). You see, faith affected the way he lived in one of the most godless societies ever recorded. (See Genesis 6.)

Now, how can I please God? "And without faith it is impossible to please God, because anyone who comes to him must believe that he exists and that he rewards those who earnestly seek him" (verse 6 NIV). Two things:

- We must believe he exists.
- We must believe he rewards those who genuinely seek him.

How can I do this? Believe. It is important to understand that *faith* and *believe* are the same word in the Bible. One is a noun, *faith* (the Greek word is *pistis*). The other is a verb, *believe* (the Greek word is *pisteuo*).

Here is where the light came on for me, my aha moment. The Bible says that it is impossible for God to lie (Hebrews 6:18). Therefore, I understand that God's Word is true, and I can trust it to always be true. If God said it, the only things that remains is, "Will I believe it?"

Concerning my salvation, I have peace because he said, "Everyone who calls on the name of the Lord will be saved" (Romans 10:13 NIV). I believe it. He promised, "God has said, 'Never will I leave you; never will I forsake you'" (Hebrews 13:5 NIV). His list of promises goes on continually.

I know of only one way to live victoriously in this world: Believe what God says in his word. "Everyone born of God overcomes the world. This is the victory that has overcome the world, even our faith. Who is it that overcomes the world? Only the one who believes that Jesus is the Son of God" (1 John 5:4–5 NIV).

We must know what God says. We must understand what he says. Then we can believe what he says. Then, victory is promised. This is the faith that never fails. Do we believe?

CHAPTER 5

FAITH THAT IS FLAWED

Dr. Arthur Williams was my pastor. He was a retired Bible instructor from Cedarville University, a Christian college of the arts and sciences, where he had taught in the 1960s. In fact, there is still a building (once a dormitory) that bears his name. Ironically, while he was in his eighties, I became his pastor.

During his tenure as an instructor, he playfully proclaimed, "Don't call me a professor. Call me a possessor!" He wanted to underscore the fact that he did not merely profess faith in Christ; He possessed faith in our Savior.

When a person possesses genuine faith, there is remarkable evidence seen in the way that he lives. In the New Testament, we learn that *faith* and *love* are synonymous. Here are four key passages worthy of memorization:

The only thing that counts is faith expressing itself through love. (Galatians 5:6 NIV)

Keeping God's commands is what counts. (1 Corinthians 7:19 NIV)

What are his commands?

> A new command I give you: Love one another. As I have loved you, so you must love one another. By this

> everyone will know that you are my disciples, if you love one another. (John 13:34–35 NIV)

> And this is his command: to believe in the name of his Son, Jesus Christ, and to love one another as he commanded us. (1 John 3:23 NIV)

When love is removed from the equation, we will discover a faith that is flawed. The brother of our Lord Jesus was greatly disturbed by the "professors" of faith in his day who did not keep Jesus's commands. In James 2:14–17, we read,

> "What good is it, my brothers and sisters, if someone claims to have faith but has no deeds? Can such faith save them? Suppose a brother or a sister is without clothes and daily food. If one of you says to them, 'Go in peace; keep warm and well fed,' but does nothing about their physical needs, what good is it? In the same way, faith by itself, if it is not accompanied by action, is dead" (NIV).

> The disciple who spoke of love in his writings more than anyone else agreed with James. "If anyone has material possessions and sees a brother or sister in need but has no pity on them, how can the love of God be in that person? Dear children, let us not love with words or speech but with actions and in truth" (1 John 3:17–18 NIV).

James made it clear that if our faith does not translate in our attitude and outreach to other people, our faith is as flawed as the demons! "But someone will say, 'You have faith; I have deeds.' Show me your faith without deeds, and I will show you my faith by my deeds. You believe that there is one God. Good! Even the demons believe that—and shudder" (James 2:18–19 NIV). We can have our theology right, but if it doesn't change our lives, it is useless.

This is an issue that is either black or white in Scripture. Has my relationship with Christ changed my relationship with people? I will admit that there have been people in my life that I have had difficulty loving. Even so, through faith, I understand that loving someone has nothing to do with accepting their behavior, trusting them, or even entering a friendship with them. It has everything to do with loving them enough to pray for them and accepting them as people loved by our Savior and even reaching out to them if a need arises.

The apostle Paul expressed our changed lives this way, "Therefore, if anyone is in Christ, the new creation has come: The old has gone, the new is here!" (2 Corinthians 5:17 NIV). As I think about my walk with Christ, I can mark many things that have changed almost instantaneously and others that more slowly evolved.

Loving others has probably been my slowest area of spiritual growth. I understood very little about the greatest commandment, let alone the second greatest. "'Love the Lord your God with all your heart and with all your soul and with all your mind.' This is the first and greatest commandment. And the second is like it: 'Love your neighbor as yourself'" (Matthew 22:38–39 NIV).

I heard my pastor say that his list of rules to live by had grown shorter the longer he lived, and now it was down to only two: The Great Commandment and the second great one. I finally understood how essential it is that we must love God above all and to love others as I love myself.

And therein lies the rub. I did not love myself. I never had. I discovered I was an extremely selfish person who sought to please only me. It led me down a desperate path of self-destruction and caused me to wound many hearts indiscriminately. I was too worn-out and frayed by carrying a huge burden of guilt to really care much about others.

My bitterness and anger with God for making me into such a creature melted away the day I realized the person I had become was not God's fault. It was all my fault because of the choices I had made. In repentance for not only my choices, but also my attitude, my guilt fell away.

Something strange happened that day. I stopped hating myself. As time progressed, I began liking, then loving the person he made me to be. I stopped regretting my past and became thankful for the person he made me to be.

And a new dimension opened in my heart. It took a while to recognize what was going on, but I became aware that, surprisingly, I could and did love other people. Reaching out to offer hope to hurting hearts is only one way of expressing my love. This love thing is so multifaceted!

CHAPTER 6

THE FAITH THAT FREES US

Twelve-step groups have been both an astounding success and a colossal failure. I know people who have scoffed at Alcoholics Anonymous as well as those who cling to both the group and the precepts by which they govern their daily lives. There are probably as many twelve-step groups available as there are addictions that enslave the soul and body of men and women. The site 12step.org lists the steps in generic form. Let's look at the first three.

> Step 1: We admitted that we were powerless over our addiction—that our lives have become unmanageable.
>
> Step 2: Came to believe that a Power greater than ourselves could restore us to sanity.
>
> Step 3: Made a decision to turn our will and our lives over to the care of God as we understood God.

I have heard those inside the program say that these first three steps can keep a person sober. I would say, based on personal experience, success depends upon in Whom I place my faith and the degree to which I trust him. The God in Whom I have placed my faith has promised victory. My life is a growing process of believing him.

In our journey of discovering faith, we have learned that two words are synonymous: *faith* (a noun) and *believe* (a verb). It helps my understanding for me to say, "Faith is believing God. God said it. I believe it. That settles it!"

Secondly, we have uncovered that faith is revealed in our actions. To put this in the simplest terms I know, "Love is faith in action!" I believe Jesus died to pay for my sins and he promised to give me eternal life. That eternal life does not begin the day I die. No! It began the day I accepted him as my Savior.

Now, as a child of God, an heir of God, and a joint heir with Jesus, I am capable of loving as he commanded. But why, oh, why, do I feel so defeated? If faith is the victory that overcomes the world, why do I feel like such a loser?

Are you like me? Do you say, "I beg God every day to take the sinful desire away! I plead with him to give me victory, but it never comes! I feel like 'I succeed just often enough to be a flop as a failure!'?" (Charles Schultz's *Peanuts* character, Charlie Brown).

Whatever you have in your mouth right now, take it out! Let's not bite any pencils in two or suck ink into our lungs or rip off a fingernail. We need to grasp one important all-inclusive truth:

> ***God never told us to beg for anything. He only asks that we believe him!***

What are we to believe? "This is the victory that has overcome the world, even our faith. Who is it that over-comes the world? Only the one who believes that Jesus is the Son of God" (1 John 5:4–5 NIV). Have we placed our faith in Christ? Yes? Then we have the victory!

"We are more than conquerors through him who loved us" (Romans 8:37 NIV). "More than conquerors" is one word in the original language. I think we can relate to this literally today: "We are 'hyper' winners!" What is better than being a winner? Being a "hyper winner"! But do we believe that we are? If so, let's stop looking at ourselves as losers!

"But, Charlie, why do I struggle with defeat so much? I am faced with issues in my life that are so hard. Sometimes I fold like a house of cards in a breeze. I don't think I have addiction problems, but there are things I just keep doing. I can withstand anything but temptation." It is strange how a negative perspective of ourselves, a loser mentality, sets us up to fail. If we view ourselves as losers, we will continue to fail.

Jesus said, "Very truly I tell you, everyone who sins is a slave to sin" (John 8:34 NIV). I'm thinking, "Yeah, that's what I'm thinking." But that is not all Jesus said in this passage. "To the Jews who had believed him, Jesus said, 'If you hold to my teaching, you are really my disciples. Then you will know the truth, and the truth will set you free… So if the Son sets you free, you will be free indeed'" (John 8:31, 32, 36 NIV). What did he teach? Believe him and love one another.

Here is what we are told happens in the life of those who believe in Jesus. Faith in him promotes obedience to his word and sets us free from the bondage of slavery to sin. Free, really, truly free through faith in our Savior. Don't say, "Yes, but…" Stop making excuses. Stop begging. Believe! I am free!

I never needed to talk God into helping me. The truth is, in my humanity, I don't have the ability to win the battles. I was trying to get God to give me what I already had! Me? Can't do it! Him? It's done through Christ. He says so lovingly, "Charlie, believe Me."

What is it that sets (present tense) us free? The truth. What is that? When Jesus prayed for his disciples and those who would believe through them, he asked the Father, "Sanctify them by the truth; your word is truth" (John 17:17 NIV).

Our journey through the studies presented in this book is my attempt to present the truth an understandable way. The "secrets of the blessed" are totally ineffective if the truth is not believed, but life changing if they are. The same can be said about your pastor's messages or Sunday school class or the small group Bible study you might attend.

When you pick up your Bible to read it, seek to under-stand what it means and believe what God reveals to you. Our Father never designed the new life in Christ to be a miserable, defeated, guilt-ridden existence. He never meant for our walk with him to feel so impossible.

CHAPTER 7

FAITH FOR LIVING

I have never been able to be good enough to be happy. On the other side of the coin, I've never been bad enough to be happy either. Well, I have tried a lot harder to be good, but no matter how much effort I put in it, I failed to be good or happy. That's a sad admission.

As sad as my admission may be, I find among God's people something that is equally sad. People whole love our Lord and faithfully serve him express having no assurance of their salvation. The best they can say is, "I hope I'll make it, but I guess I'll just have to wait and see." But please hear what God has to say, "I write these things to you who believe in the name of the Son of God so that you may know that you have eternal life" (1 John 5:13–14 NIV).

In an effort to find happiness, I carefully kept my glaring weaknesses hidden from most of the people who knew me. I thought maybe I could better manage my behavior if I added more controls. So, my list of rules got longer and longer—you know, the things I must not do as well as the good things that surely would strengthen me.

I made goals for reading the Bible through in a year. One year, I pledged to read the New Testament through once a month. I didn't make it every month, but it was a rich experience to read it through six times. I read Christian books voraciously. I attended all church services and went to every Christian conference I could.

None of these good things—and so many more I haven't mentioned ever—brought lasting happiness. I blamed it all on my private hidden sin, an area of my life I allowed no one to see. But why didn't the good things help me conquer the bad? I was miserable.

Okay, now that I have made these admissions to you, I must quickly add that I do not believe our Heavenly Father ever meant for our walk with him to be difficult or unhappy. But as I observe believers around me, I think there are a lot of struggling Christians plodding through a somewhat dismal existence.

Why is this so? I'm sure there is not a one-size-fits-all answer. However, on four separate occasions, God reduces our lives with Him in the simplest terms possible.

"But the righteous will live by his faith" (Habakkuk 2:4, NASB). Habakkuk was perplexed because God said he was going to use the wicked Babylonians to bring Judah back to himself. As the prophet questioned him, God said, "Don't worry about that. Live by faith!" That is good advice for us to follow when we don't understand what God is doing. God is simply saying, "Trust me, even when you don't understand me."

"For in the gospel the righteousness of God is revealed—a righteousness that is by faith from first to last, just as it is written: 'The righteous will live by faith'" (Romans 1:17 NIV). First to last and everything in between, we live by faith—not works, not by trying to be good enough.

"Clearly no one who relies on the law is justified before God, because 'the righteous will live by faith'" (Galatians 3:11 NIV). The context declares that we cannot be good enough to be righteous.

If we could, we would have to keep all the law perfectly and we would not need Christ.

"But my righteous one will live by faith" (Hebrews 10:38 NIV). Literally, God's righteous ones are not quitters. Here's the big question: "How do you become one of God's righteous ones?" Obviously, we cannot be "good enough" because we all sin, and the "wages of sin is death" (Romans 6:23, KJV).

The answer is Christ and the price he paid for our sins on the cross. "God made him who had no sin to be sin for us, so that in him we might become the righteousness of God" (2 Corinthians 5:21 NIV). Look at this verse closely. He never sinned, yet the Father made him to be sin for us. Why? So, we might become the righteousness of God!

> **Let me state this another way: *He became as sinful as we are so that we might become as righteous as he is*!**

This is not something I can earn This is what I must believe. This is what he gave me the moment I was saved. "Therefore, since we have been justified [literally: declared righteous] through faith, we have peace with God through our Lord Jesus Christ" (Romans 5:1 NIV).

Someone might say, "If I believed what you are saying, I would go out and sin all I want!" Quite frankly, I do believe this is the truth revealed in the Scriptures, and I sin more than I want!

My righteousness depends solely on Christ. Remember, *faith* means "believing God." Loving one another is faith in action. This faith sets us free to live victoriously with Christ. Now I find myself freed from the performance trap of trying to keep a list of rules to try to please God.

We live by faith, and faith affects the way we live. "You, my brothers and sisters, were called to be free. But do not use your freedom to indulge the flesh; rather, serve one another humbly in love. For the entire law is fulfilled in keeping this one command: 'Love your neighbor as yourself'" (Galatians 5:13–14 NIV).

So, what does this mean? What difference will this make in my life? First, it means I have choices. I can choose to believe the lies in my head, which are telling me how bad I am, or I can choose to believe what God has said about any given situation. Am I really a no-good rotten sinner—something God never says about his children—or am I a blood-bought child of God?

I can choose to live as a slave to my desires or as a servant of righteousness, as Paul taught in Romans 6. I can identify with Paul's misery in the battle to do right in Romans 7 or live the joy he claimed in 8:1–2, "Therefore, there is now no condemnation for those who are in Christ Jesus, because through Christ Jesus the law of the Spirit who gives life has set you free from the law of sin and death" (NIV).

I have learned to quit trying to fight the war Jesus had already won. It has amazed me the peace and joy that has enveloped my being since accepting that my sole responsibility is to believe him. Even if I sin, forgiveness is only a whispered prayer away. By faith, I know Jesus paid for all my sins, even the ones I have yet to commit, when he died on the cross and rose from the dead.

You and I are his righteous children. Now, we live by faith. It's time to be happy!

CHAPTER 8

FAITH: IS SEEING REALLY BELIEVING?

After preaching what I thought was a positive, uplifting message titled "Faith Is the Victory," asad, strugglingg mom spoke to me as she left the service, saying, "You don't know how bad sermons like that make me feel." It was a sobering realization that I had totally missed the mark of meeting this lady's needs.

That was almost thirty years ago, but I still mull it over in my mind from time to time. I came to understand her better when I finally admitted I felt the same way she did. I've heard it stated many times by other folks who confessed, "I guess I just don't have enough faith." We all look around and agree that maybe if we had more faith, we would see our prayers answered or see God moving in our world.

It has been my goal to offer hope to hurting people so we may gain courage to live by faith. I suppose any attempt to be a blessing has fallen short of being helpful when we are left feeling like our faith is insufficient for our needs. Perhaps you are like me and have thought, "If only God would prove himself to me, then I could believe." We have learned that faith is believing God; "God said it, I believe it, that settles it for me." Genuine faith reveals itself by how we treat others: "By this shall all men know you are my disciples if you love one another." This faith that directs our lives frees us to love and serve our God.

Let's take a few moments to consider biblical history. Maybe we have thought, "If only I could feel God's presence, then I could believe." Adam walked with God every evening, yet crashed and burned when tempted to disobey God. He lived in a perfect, sinless state, but "seeing was not believing" for him.

Abraham was visited personally by the angel the Lord, a personification of God himself. In his visible form, he promised that the nations would come from his descendants. Yet, as God was molding Abraham into a man of faith, twice he feared so much for his life, he ordered his wife to lie and say she was his sister.

While talking to God personally, first his doubts concerning the promises sought to make his chief servant's son the heir of the promise. When he was told he would have a son of his own, he took matters into his own hands and impregnated his wife's servant girl. For fourteen years, he thought Ishmael was the promised son until God declared that Sarah would be a mother at age ninety.

The nation of Israel, Abraham's offspring, saw God's hand in the ten plagues against Egypt. They saw God blow back the Red Sea, walked through it on dry ground, and witnessed Pharaoh's army drown. He appeared to them as a pillar of fire at night and a pillar of cloud by day. He gave them water out of a rock and fed them with manna every day, a miracle food.

All this "seeing is believing," yet when they spied out the Promised Land, their hearts melted in them. The spies came back with a "good news, bad news" report. The good news: the land is productive and blessed, just as God had promised. The bad news: There are giants in the land! We felt like grasshoppers next to them! We can't conquer this land! It's impossible!

Their courage, instead of being like iron, became like water. They intended to elect a new leader who would take them back to Egypt. Despite all they had seen, their unbelief resulted in forty years of wandering in the desert, and everyone above the age twenty (except for the two spies who believed: Joshua and Caleb) died in the wilderness.

There are Bible stories about people who needed special encouragement, and God did give them a sign to bolster their faith. I'm thinking of Gideon's "fleece." I've heard of people who believe this is still a good way to discern God's will. If you do, then I suggest you use a real fleece. Put a cotton ball on the ground and ask God to make it dry while the ground is wet and then reverse it the next day!

Perhaps the clearest example of "seeing is believing" given in Scripture is the story of doubting Thomas.

> Now Thomas (also known as Didymus, one of the Twelve, was not with the disciples when Jesus came. So the other disciples told him, "We have seen the Lord!" But he said to them, "Unless I see the nail marks in his hands and put my finger where the nails were, and put my hand into his side, I will not believe." A week later his disciples were in the house again, and Thomas was with them. Though the doors were locked, Jesus came and stood among them and said, "Peace be with you!" Then he said to Thomas, "Put your finger here; see my hands. Reach out your hand and put it into my side. Stop doubting and believe." Thomas said to him, "My Lord and my God!" Then Jesus told him, "Because you have seen me, you have believed; blessed are those who have not seen and yet have believed." (John 20:24–29 NIV)

Jesus tells us the real blessing is believing without proof, without needing to see first. If we revisit Hebrews 11 for a moment, we can discover that faith is not a response to proof, but rather faith is a response to promise. Noah lived in a wicked world, and God told him about things he had never seen before: rain. Not only that, but enough rain to flood the world. Beyond that, he was told to build a boat to save his family, and he was moved by fear (belief in what was to come) and obeyed.

With all his struggles concerning his descendants, God told Abraham to pack up; leave home, friends, and family; and move. Abraham did so without knowing where he was going because God had promised to lead him to a land. Concerning a child, God waited until Abraham was impotent and Sarah was past menopause, but they both believed they would receive the promise. Through faith, the impossible became possible because they believed God.

God had promised that this child, Isaac, would become the father of a nation as numerous as the stars in heaven. Yet when God told him to offer Isaac as a human sacrifice, Abraham did not hesitate because he believed God's promise to the point that God would raise Isaac from the dead.

The list goes on. Each person believed the promise of God without requiring proof.

> All these people were still living by faith when they died. They did not receive the things promised; they only saw them and welcomed them from a distance, admitting that they were foreigners and strangers on earth. (Hebrews 11:13–14 NIV)

> These were all commended for their faith, yet none of them received what had been promised, since God had planned something better for us so that only together with us would they be made perfect. (Hebrews 11:39–40 NIV)

Many of our promises are given to us in future tense. Heaven, the return of Christ, a new eternal home, a glorified body, beholding the face of Jesus—these are all things we look forward to.

Many promises we experience right now. Our sins are forgiven through Christ. We have peace with God. We talk with our God, and he listens and answers our prayers. Books are written naming the promises of God.

Does our God offer us proof? Every moment of every day, we can see him at work if we are watching through the eyes that believe him. Instead of moaning our lack of faith, it is entirely within our power to choose to believe his promises. He has recorded his promises in a very convenient place.

We call it our Bible. God's Book of Promises.

PART 2

STRUGGLING WITH DOUBT

CHAPTER 9

ADMITTING DOUBT

Followers of Jesus Christ accept him as their Savior by faith. That is the way it is supposed to be. We believe the Bible to be the Word of God, and he says, "Believe on the Lord Jesus Christ and you will be saved." It was this simple statement that brought peace to my soul many years ago. Some may consider this to be "blind faith." I am not certain what that means, but I do know believers who seldom struggle with doubt. Still, there are others who at one time or another have fought aggressively against it. I am one who wrestled long and hard with such conflicting thoughts.

As strange as it may seem, many doubts surfaced after years of being a Christian. What are we to do? We cower from the thought of *doubt*. Often, we are afraid to admit we have any because Christians aren't supposed to doubt. It is true that Jesus taught his disciples that to doubt was to express unbelief (Matthew 14:31). James said that anyone who doubted was unstable and should not expect answers to their prayers (James 1:6). Romans 14:23 says, "Everything that does not come from faith is sin" (NIV).

We live in a world of people who demand that we adopt their beliefs. The philosophy teacher may demand a in "no absolutes" or "situational ethics" or even "no god. "Hell, fire, and brimstone" preachers proclaim a God of condemnation and fear, creating a doubt that God really loves us. A college student is taught to abandon his faith while other Christians are lulled into complacency by a pulpit that offers few challenges. Perhaps you know someone whose faith was damaged by one of these circumstances.

The truth of the matter is, we do doubt. What can we do about it? May I ask, "Do we know why we believe what we believe?"? If we don't know, how can we expect to conquer our misgivings?

I struggled with my own deep personal despair from my misunderstanding of what I believed to be the "unfairness of God." I often described feeling like a pawn in a super- natural chess game between God and Satan. I considered myself an abused child of God. Why did God make me the way that I am? My pain and despair drove me to question if God was real, why didn't he hear me? Why didn't he answer my prayers? Why didn't he care?

Life has a way of promoting doubts with the passage of time and circumstances. My experience resulted in a deep-seated anger in which I emptied my venom verbally at God. It does little good to hold inside what God already knows. Looking back, I can honestly say it was like the child who tells his parent, "I hate you!" The parent says wisely, "That's too bad because I love you more than you can imagine."

Of course, by telling myself I should not doubt—because doubting is sin—I created a burden of guilt. I'd muster up as much faith as I could and try again. It was like trying to run a spiritual potato-sack race. With my feet in the bag, I'd reach down and pull up the top of my faith bag and start hopping! I didn't get far until I fell again. I tried so hard so many times, I finally fell without the will to get up again.

Obviously, something changed in my heart. Would it surprise you to know that the Bible records several prominent people who doubted God? If you relate in any way to what I have shared, I'd like to investigate characters who overcame their doubts by God's grace and became true spiritual heroes.

CHAPTER 10

WHEN GOD FAILS TO MEET OUR EXPECTATIONS

Phillip Yancey wrote a book he entitled *Disappointment with God* (Zondervan, 1988). Some people were offended by the title, but I grabbed it immediately and devoured it mentally. I read it several times and highlighted many portions and made notes in the margins. It was a breath of fresh air for me to know there were other people who had issues with their concept of God.

Not too many years later, "Focus on the Family" founder, James Dobson, wrote *When God Doesn't Make Sense* (Tyndale House Publishers, 1993). Again, it was like a cold drink of water to a thirsty soul. I highly recommend these two books to those who struggle with doubt. I have loaned my copies out more times than I can remember.

During my years of struggle, I felt these two books freed me to admit my struggles. I certainly did not understand God, and I was severely disappointed in him. I had tried to know him better. I read the Bible through many times. I read hundreds of spiritual books and periodicals. I tuned in Christian radio constantly and listen to the famous Bible teachers of yesterday and today. I prayed. Oh, how I prayed. But it seemed that God just didn't listen. My life fell apart, not because of the mistakes, but because of bad choices I felt powerless to deny.

It was during this time of spiritual drought while still struggling for answers, while trying to pray, it seemed like I heard a voice speak in my mind. It said, "Can you believe me, even if you don't understand me? Will you trust me, even if I fail to meet your expectations?" I said, "Yes, Lord." Though the war was not over, a battle was won.

Much like myself, Abraham was a man who had to struggle through the times when it seemed God just wasn't keeping his promises. Here is how his story unfolded.

> The Lord had said to Abram, "Go from your country, your people and your father's household to the land I will show you. I will make you into a great nation, and I will bless you; I will make your name great, and you will be a blessing. I will bless those who bless you, and whoever curses you I will curse; and all Peoples on earth will be blessed through you." (Genesis 12:1–3 NIV)

Imagine getting a message from God to pack up your family and move. My first question would have been, "Where?" God says, "I'll tell you when you get there!" I must admit, in my mind, Abraham had a lot of faith to even start the journey!

God repeats his promise in one way or another four more times. "I'm going to build a great nation from you with descendants the stars in the sky. They will inherit this land as far as you can see!" (Genesis 12:7; 13:14–17; paraphrase). After a great military victory, "The Lord came to Abram in a vision: 'Do not be afraid, Abram. I am your shield, your very great reward'" (15:1 NIV). "But Abram said, 'Sovereign Lord, what can you give me since I remain childless and the one who will inherit my estate is Eliezer of Damascus?' And Abram said, 'You have given me no children; so a servant in my household will be my heir'" (15:2–3 NIV).

Here he is, past seventy-five years old, and his only option for an heir is to follow the middle eastern custom of making his head servant's son his heir.

The Lord says, "No way! You are going to be a daddy, and that child will be your heir." (Forgive my loose paraphrasing, please.) Again, God shares the details of the promise. Scripture records Abraham's response so clearly: "Abram believed the Lord, and he credited it to him as righteousness" (verse 6 NIV). This outstanding statement is used by the apostle Paul to argue that we are saved through faith alone, completely apart from works (Romans 4:3, Galatians 3:6).

Still, time dragged on. Still, no baby.

Forgetting these promises, Abraham lied to two kings because he was afraid he would be murdered so his wife could be taken into the king's harem. If God hasn't yet kept this one promise for a baby, perhaps he found it tough to trust God for his safety. Was Abraham so real that he might have said, "Honey, we are in the waiting room waiting for God to give us a family. You're a beautiful lady. I'm afraid for my life. Please just tell people you are my sister."

This isn't all. He accepted his wife's suggestion that he father a baby with her servant girl. You know, Abraham lived fourteen years believing the baby boy was the heir to the promises before he learned Ishmael was not the chosen child. He had gotten ahead of God, trying to manipulate circumstances. Sometimes I am guilty of thinking the same way, "God needs my help to get this done." The truth of the matter is, God doesn't need me at all, but like Abraham, he may choose to use me.

Why do we have to wait? God has his reasons, which are undoubtedly beyond our ability to understand. For me, I learned that I first needed to accept where I was and who I was without seeing even the evidence of God's answer. It was then my heart discovered the peace only God can give. "Do not be anxious about anything, but in every situation, by prayer and petition, with thanksgiving, present your requests to God. And the peace of God, which transcends all understanding, will guard your hearts and your minds in Christ Jesus" (Philippians 4:6–7 NIV).

This is an issue of accepting our lives on God's terms. I can hear someone say, "Charlie, you don't know how messed up my life is!" True, and you don't know how messed up I was! No matter how hard I tried, I could not change my heart. Only God could.

In Philippians, Paul tells us the remedy for our anxieties is prayer with thanksgiving. The giving of thanks is the acknowledgement on our part of the acceptance of our circumstances. "Thank You, God, that I am Charlie. Thank You for loving me completely with all my flaws. Thank You that You have a plan to change me into the image of Christ." The longer we hold our anger, bitterness, or anxiety about how things are versus how we want them to be, the longer we will postpone peace in our hearts.

In our next lesson on struggling with doubt, a man named Asaph will teach us some more.

CHAPTER 11

WHEN GOD ISN'T FAIR

Even though I am an adult, I still find it easy to play the "Not fair!" card when things don't go my way. I'm still growing in my walk with Jesus, and this response does not happen very often anymore, but there was a time when it formed a major obstacle in my life.

We all have major flaws in our character because we are human and inherited them from our earthly father, Adam. Some of these character defects are obvious, others are not easily recognized. Still, we all have them. It's called our sin nature. Someone aptly said, "We are all made from mud. Some of us are just muddier than others!"

When the Holy Spirit convicts us, we beg God to take it or them away, but he doesn't. We struggle to overcome, but it seems the harder we try, the deeper into the hole of despair we fall. And it just doesn't seem fair. We look at others and believe they have it all together. They don't seem to struggle at all. Or perhaps there are others who do things we consider even worse, but with no conscience or consequences. It just isn't fair that we are so miserable.

Asaph is one of those lesser-known characters in the Old Testament. He is the writer of twelve Psalms. That is all we really know about him. In Psalm 73, he bares his soul as he expresses his frustration at the unfairness of life.

> Surely God is good to Israel, to those who are pure in heart. But as for me, my feet had almost slipped; I had nearly lost my foothold. For I envied the arrogant when I saw the prosperity of the wicked. (Psalm 73:1–3 NIV)

Asaph wrote during a time of visible evidence of God's goodness to the nation of Israel. Yet when he looked in the other direction at the prosperity of the godless compared to his own poverty, he found himself on the slippery slope of jealousy. Life just wasn't fair.

In the next several verses, he described the character of these arrogant people. They were healthy and did not carry the burdens that other people did. They were proud and mistreated others. With calloused hearts, they perpetrated acts of violence. They scoffed, spoke with words intended to hurt, and made threats to oppress the weaker.

In verse 12, he says, "This is what the wicked are like—always free of care, they go on amassing wealth" (NIV). Asaph took all this very hard. Maybe you've been there. You struggle to make ends meet, but the neighbor next door is rolling in cash. You can't afford the repairs on your old car, but your boss pulls up in a brand-new Lexus.

Maybe you have an addiction that you fight against, and you suffer such horrible guilt. Why won't God set you free? Hey, I'm with you on all accounts. Like Asaph, I had to change the way I thought. I needed a new perspective, call it an attitude adjustment!

> Surely in vain I have kept my heart pure and have washed my hands in innocence. All day long I have been afflicted, and every morning brings new punishments.

> If I had spoken out like that, I would have betrayed your children. When I tried to understand all this, it troubled me deeply till I entered the sanctuary of God; then I understood their final destiny. (Verses 13–17 NIV)

He saw what he had instead of what he didn't have. He no longer doubted the goodness of his God. He no longer saw life or God as being unfair. Why? Because there is more to life than things, health, or fairness. He saw life from the point of view of his relationship with his Heavenly Father. He had a genuine acceptance of himself and his circumstances.

About eighteen years ago, I learned that my sinful nature was complicated by a chemical imbalance in my brain. I have bipolar disorder. Notice, I did not say I am bipolar. I am so much more. I am a child of God with a disorder. I'll not go into detail, but prior to the diagnosis, I had no idea why I had such irrational thoughts and behavior. Talk about feeling life was unfair! Why had God made me this way? I do not blame the disorder because I know I am still to this day responsible for my choices. But, I reasoned, God could have made me normal (whatever that is!).

I doubted God's love for me. I cried for healing that never came. I prayed for deliverance he never gave. Some have testimonies of miraculous change, but I do not. The personal cost was heavy, but it was even worse for those who loved me. It was so unfair to all involved.

But over time, my thinking changed, even to the point that I can now say I am blessed to have bipolar disorder. Since I know what it is like, and I am learning constantly how to manage it, maybe I can help someone else along the way.

I cannot pinpoint a specific moment when this change came about, but I do remember laying hold to Romans 8:28, "And we know that in all things God works for the good of those who love him, who have been called according to his purpose" (NIV). I began believing, "God meant this for my good."

No one ever promised that life would be fair. We live in a fallen world, should we expect anything different? But hey! What about the struggles with that old sinful nature? They are not over, but I now recognize that I am the winner through Christ, who loves me (Romans 8:37).

CHAPTER 12

HOW CAN I KNOW I AM SAVED?

Doubt comes in many ways. I suppose the most pervasive and unsettling form is the question, "Am I really a Christian?" We have an adversary who loves to whisper in our ears all sorts of accusations to convince us that we are not truly a child of God. If we step out of line in some way, the plague of guilt weighs us down.

Through the years, I have met many Christians who have struggled over this question. I'll be blunt: I think the deceiver has the wrong people doubting their salvation. I've seen people of faith living good lives and serving Christ faithfully, but they struggle desperately while others who outwardly demonstrate no evidence of salvation are not bothered at all. I'm glad that God looks at our hearts, and he alone is capable of judging.

We appeal to lost people to receive Christ as their Savior. We emphasize that we must repent of our sins. We repeat the words of Jesus, "You must be born again!" (John 3:7 NIV). We quote the Scriptures and say, "Everyone who calls on the name of the Lord will be saved" (Romans 10:13 NIV). We lead people in the sinner's prayer.

And we are right. This is all true. Repeatedly, though, I have found a common thread among people who have been raised in the church from infancy. There are some who do not remember a time they received Christ as their Savior. They cannot recall a time in which they did not believe.

I remember the first time I encountered this as I interviewed a woman for church membership who shared this experience. She had been tormented by this lack of a spiritual birthday and sought counsel from many pastors who all led her through the sinner's prayer. All those prayers brought her no peace.

Finally, she met a pastor who asked, "What do you believe right now?" She believed Jesus died and was raised again to give her the forgiveness of sins and eternal life. She believed the gospel! With that realization, the matter was settled in her heart.

Did you know there is no sinner's prayer in the Bible? The closest we come to such was when the tax collector prayed, "God, have mercy on me, a sinner" (Luke 18:13 NIV).

When the Lord brought me to himself, no one led me to Christ. I didn't pray. I didn't know what to pray. Convicted of my sins, I responded to an invitation at my very informal church. I knelt at the altar and was joined by dozens of people praying for me. I had no peace until my brother-in-law said, "Just believe!" I rose to my feet and someone asked, "Do you believe?" I said, "Yes." God spoke peace to my heart.

Later, as a new believer, I struggled with yielding to temptation. Also, I began hearing those heart wrenching questions, and I doubted. I had no sinner's prayer, nor did I call audibly on the name of the Lord. As I prayed and meditated on the Scriptures concerning salvation, I realized I did call on the Lord in my heart. He promised that if I did, I would be saved. It was not a matter of feeling saved, it was the fact of being saved because he promised he would do it. He cannot break a promise. He cannot lie (Hebrews 6:18).

What must we believe to be saved? This is the question the Philippian jailer asked Paul. He answered, "Believe in the Lord Jesus, and you will be saved" (Acts 16:31 NIV). Peter tells us, "Salvation is found in no one else, for there is no other name under heaven given to mankind by which we must be saved" (Acts 4:12 NIV).

Paul shares with us the Gospel in a nutshell:

> Now, brothers and sisters, I want to remind you of the gospel I preached to you, which you received and on which you have taken your stand. By this gospel you are saved, if you hold firmly to the word I preached to you. Otherwise, you have believed in vain. For what I received I passed on to you as of first importance: that Christ died for our sins according to the Scriptures, that he was buried, that he was raised on the third day according to the Scriptures. (1 Corinthians 15:1–4 NIV)

It's not complicated. What do you believe now? Do you believe Christ died for your sin? Do you believe he was raised again from the dead on the third day?

Do you believe on the Lord Jesus Christ and trusting in him alone for salvation apart from anything you do? There is no room for "Yes, but…"

> For it is by grace you have been saved, through faith—and this is not from yourselves, it is the gift of God—not by works, so that no one can boast. (Ephesians 2:8–9 NIV)

Do you believe?

It is customary to say thank-you after receiving a gift. Regardless how you feel right now, bow your head, close your eyes, and say, "Thank you, Lord, for saving my soul!" Keep saying it until you mean it.

CHAPTER 13

THE CURE FOR DOUBT

Everyone has faith. By that, I mean, everyone believes something, even if they claim to believe nothing (that is the belief in unbelief—think about it)! Being a "spiritual person" is very popular today. That term covers a lot of bases, including having faith in faith itself. The big question is, "What do I believe?" or "In whom do I believe?"

Again, I must speak from my personal experience. Not only did I struggle with my relationship with God, but in my darkest hours, I wondered if I really believed the right things. Was the God I claimed to know real? Does he even exist? What if the atheist is correct? I set out in my own private pursuit of truth.

I have become convinced that I can never truly understand my position until I understand the position of those with whom I do not agree. I think I am in good company because Solomon did the same search: "I, the Teacher, was king over Israel in Jerusalem. I applied my mind to study and to explore by wisdom all that is done under the heavens. What a heavy burden God has laid on mankind! I have seen all the things that are done under the sun; all of them are meaningless, a chasing after the wind" (Ecclesiastes 1:12 NIV).

Solomon found his investigation to be a waste of time. Why? I honestly don't know, but perhaps it was because of the way he approached his research. He married hundreds of wives, and Scripture tells us they turned his heart away from the Lord. For him, all was meaningless. The only hint that his pursuit of wisdom brought him back to God is in Ecclesiastes 12:13–14: "Now all has been heard; here is the conclusion of the matter: Fear God and keep his commandments, for this is the duty of all mankind. For God will bring every deed into judgment, including every hidden thing, whether it is good or evil" (NIV).

Like many other believers in Christ, I needed answers to questions that troubled me. When a person shares that they are struggling with doubt, I think it can be a good thing. Doubt is not just a heart issue, but it is also a matter of the mind. What we think becomes what we believe. It makes sense then that if we change the way we think, we can deal effectively with our doubts. By intellectual exploration of a subject from all possible sides, bathing it in prayer, a person may discover the truth and be stronger for it.

Some think that Christians must "check their brain at the door" to believe in God. For many people, science provides all the answers they need. Others find science substantiates creation rather than evolution. Your conclusion may be different from mine, but my inquiry resulted in a faith stronger than ever before.

The internal pain I suffered caused me to doubt God was even there. In my anger, I said, "Okay, if there is no God, what is the alternative?" I decided the only question that needed to be answered was the argument of "first cause" or what began the universe? No matter how far back I chased the beginning, the question remained, "How did it all get started?"

I could find only one answer, "In the beginning, God created." I found a fresh meaning to Hebrews 11:6: "And without faith it is impossible to please God, because anyone who comes to him must believe that he exists and that he rewards those who earnestly seek him" (NIV).

You see, it all boiled down to "what do I believe: evolution or creation?" By faith, I lay my claim on the truthfulness of God's Word. By choosing to believe God, peace settled into my soul.

As it is with any form of doubt, we must choose what we believe. Our enemy will present to us all conceivable questions to undermine the integrity of our faith. If we demand proof before we accept what God says is true, we are stepping outside the boundaries of faith. Many have been unable to take God at his word and have abandoned the faith. I have written these five chapters on doubt in hope that someone may find rest from their doubts. May God bless you in your walk with him.

PART 3

WE ALL HAVE A HISTORY

CHAPTER 14

RELEASED FROM THE GRIP OF GUILT

It amazes me that my whole life was draped on Christ as he hung on the cross. My every sin was laid upon him as he bled and died. Nothing was left out. Nothing! He didn't miss a one.

Get a grip on this fact: I had not yet sinned, but he paid for them all. My sins and your sins were all future tense. We had not yet committed any transgressions. We would not be born until some 1,900 years later. But he died for all of them. The payment for our transgressions is past tense.

Now, here is another startling fact. In the pages of Scripture, we learn that God knows everything there is to know. Nothing has ever taken him by surprise. He doesn't look down from his throne, slap himself up the side of the head, and say, "Duh, I didn't see that one coming!"

Admitting all that, it seems incredulous to think that God knew long before Calvary what a sinful mess I would make of my life, yet he chose to save me on February 5, 1967, and to forgive all my sins—even the ones I have not yet committed! There is no other way to pay for our sins. Only Christ's finished work on the cross can accomplish redemption.

The Holy Spirit moved on the writer of Hebrews to illustrate this truth:

> The law is only a shadow of the good things that are coming—not the realities themselves. For this reason, it can never, by the same sacrifices repeated endlessly year after year, make perfect those who draw near to worship. Otherwise, would they not have stopped being offered? For the worshipers would have been cleansed once for all, and would no longer have felt guilty for their sins. But those sacrifices are an annual reminder of sins. It is impossible for the blood of bulls and goats to take away sins. (10:1–4 NIV)

This is the way things were in the Old Testament. There was a consequence for sin: death. We are reminded of this in Romans 6:23, "For the wages of sin is death" (NIV). Death has always been the consequence of sin ever since Adam and Eve sinned in the Garden of Eden. Starting in the garden, the price was a blood sacrifice, the innocent dying in the place of the guilty. Because of the sin of Adam (Romans 5:12), we were born spiritually dead (Ephesians 2:1–2), doomed to die physically (Hebrews 9:27), and in danger of eternal death (Revelation 21:8).

To teach us the severity and seriousness of sin, God gave us the picture of this process in the OT Levitical priesthood. You sinned, you were required to bring a sacrifice, again, the innocent dying for the guilty. Day in, day out. Week after week. Year after year. Century after century. It never ended. There was this continual reminder that "I sinned!" Guilt was never gone.

On the Day of Atonement, the high priest would go behind the veil in the temple to offer the required sacrifice appointed by God for the sins of all the people. This he did once a year, year after year. Hebrews says that in all this, there was the constant reminder of sin. Please read this again:

> For this reason it can never, by the same sacrifices repeated endlessly year after year, make perfect those who draw near to worship. Otherwise, would they not have stopped being offered? For the worshipers would have been cleansed once for all, and would no longer have felt guilty for their sins.

You see, they always carried the burden of the guilt of their sins. These feelings of guilt still plague God's children. Even though Christ paid for our sins by taking them on his body as he suffered our punishment, we seem to forget that our debt is settled. We are forgiven. Guilt should perish, not persist.

One lady told her pastor about the guilt she carried because of an act of indiscretion.

He asked her, "Have you ever confessed this?" Her response, "Oh, pastor, a thousand times!"

"Oh, you only confessed it nine hundred ninety-nine times too many!" He reminded her that 1 John 1:9 tells us, "If we confess our sins, he is faithful and just and will forgive us our sins and purify us from all unrighteousness" (NIV).

Sin in our lives does disrupt our fellowship with God. Agreeing with God that our action was sin restores our fellowship with him. Notice, we are not told to beg, we are told to believe. This is not a perpetual motion machine to eventually relieve guilt. Forgiveness is not a feeling. It is a fact.

How does this work? Let's return to Hebrews 10:12–14: "But when this priest had offered for all time one sacrifice for sins, he sat down at the right hand of God, and since that time he waits for his enemies to be made his footstool. For by one sacrifice he has made perfect forever those who are being made holy" (NIV). Hebrews 4:14 says, "Therefore, since we have a great high priest who has ascended into heaven, Jesus the Son of God, let us hold firmly to the faith we profess" (NIV).

One sacrifice for all time.

One sacrifice for all sin.

One sacrifice for all purity: our perfection (completion).

Jesus completed his work as the High Priest, and he sat down. That is important: He sat down! All the furniture in the tabernacle in the wilderness and Solomon's temple was listed with exact instructions. But there was no chair! The priests' work was never done until Jesus finished it!

One last thing, 1 Corinthians 15:17: "And if Christ has not been raised, your faith is futile; you are still in your sins" (NIV). If Christ were still dead, he would still be paying for our sins since "the wages of sins is death." But he got up from the dead, ascended to heaven, and sat down at the right hand of the Father. His resurrection proves our sins are paid in full.

It seems too easy that we would sin and our confession bring immediate release from the quilt. We want to punish ourselves for crossing God's boundaries. We want to grieve our transgressions. However, hanging to guilt is our unbelief in the finished work of Christ. When we accept his forgiveness, we accept that "the truth will set you free" (John 8:32 NIV).

As the children sing, "Gone, gone, gone, gone! Yes! My sins are gone!"

So is my guilt!

CHAPTER 15

THANK GOD FOR YOUR STORY! THE WASTELAND OF DEPRESSION

We all have a story. My wife and I had only met a couple of weeks earlier when I told her a large portion of my story. I figured it was best to get the messy details out before we cared too deeply and found "secrets" destroying our relationship later. As I explained my history to her, I said, "The best thing you could do for yourself is to turn around and run as fast and as far as you can away from me."

She looked at me and smiled. She later said, "Your past has made you the person you are today. Who you are today is the man who I love." She blew me away with her gracious heart

Psalm 107:1–2 teaches us to be thankful for "our story." "Give thanks to the Lord, for he is good; his love endures forever. Let the redeemed of the Lord tell their story" (NIV). The writer then gives us examples of four different stories that brought shouts of praise from God's redeemed ones.

Redemption was an important concept in ancient Israel. It has to do with the payment of a debt. There were two means of debt settlement: to either sell your property or to sell yourself into slavery. If you sold your property, your children had no inheritance, hence, no home. If you sold yourself, you had no freedom.

While both were permissible under the Mosaic Law, they were not meant to be permanent. God provided two ways to end the debt. A relative could buy you or your property back from your debt holder or in the Year of Jubilee all debts were automatically cancelled and forgiven.

This paying off a debt was called redemption. It became a symbol of God paying the penalty of our sins and setting us free. The story of the Bible is when redemption finds fulfillment in the blood of our Savior: "In him we have redemption through his blood, the forgiveness of sins, in accordance with the riches of God's grace that he lavished on us" (Ephesians 1:7 NIV). Jesus paid the debt of our sins and bought us back to himself.

In Psalm 107, those whose debt have been paid are told to do something: "Let the redeemed of the Lord tell their story—those he redeemed from the hand of the foe, those he gathered from the lands, from east and west, from north and south" (NIV). So, what is your story?

The first group was those who had no direction in their lives. "Some wandered in desert wastelands, finding no way to a city where they could settle. They were hungry and thirsty, and their lives ebbed away" (107:4–5 NIV). They were wanderers. It probably didn't bother them in the beginning, but things grew old after a while.

Sooner or later, their lives became the same thing over again. They grew hungry and thirsty as they searched for a home. Each day promised more of the same. Life became a series of "if only…" After reaching the top of one hill, hoping for a sense of accomplishment, they saw more desert, more hills, more of the same scenery.

At night, they search the horizon for the glowing light of a city—in anticipation ofthe rescuee. But only darkness greeted them. Hopelessness engulfed them. The stars in the sky seemed to mock the hollowness of their hearts.

Finally, the solution filled their hearts. "Then they cried out to the Lord in their trouble, and he delivered them from their distress. He led them by a straight way to a city where they could settle" (107:67 NIV).

This desert experience easily and clearly describes my feelings at different points in my life. It is an apt depiction of depression, loneliness, and defeat that seemed to permeate my life for the longest time. While a biochemical imbalance was helped by medication, something more was needed.

You see, my thinking needed to change. I needed an attitude adjustment. That change I so desperately needed came when I "cried out to the Lord in my trouble." Hey, I hear you! You're saying, "I've been crying out for so long, I am afraid I just don't have a prayer anymore."

Let me give you some unsolicited advice from my own struggles. My oldest son wrote to me and said, "I can't pray anymore. I can't read the Bible. I can't change my heart. If God wants it done, He'll have to do it." Because I had wandered in that desert myself, God gave me life-changing instructions I could share.

"You're right. You can't change your heart. Only God can do that. Do what you can when you can. When you can pray, pray. When you can read the Word, read. But above all else, never give up." Our God is a miracle-working God. Such simple words were like seeing the glowing lights of a city in darkness of a desert night for me and my own son.

Our crying out from the depth of our needs for his intervention is the expression of faith that the god we pray to hears us and will answer. For my son and I, we had no prayer formula. No magic words to gain the attention of the Almighty. It was just believing he could and would do the impossible for us. That simple hope gave us the tenacity to not give up.

Now, something new springs up in my heart: thanksgiving. "Let them give thanks to the Lord for his unfailing love and his wonderful deeds for mankind, for he satisfies the thirsty and fills the hungry with good things" (107:8–9 NIV).

I am sharing with you a small part of my story to offer hope to those who hurt from their wandering in a desert wasteland. I give thanks to my God because he loves me enough to allow me to wander so I might share his rescue with you. My former thirsty, dry soul is satisfied with his goodness.

Being human, my natural inclination is to return to the desert of depression and despair. My cry for help is heard and, thanks again, returns to my heart.

I thank God for my story!

CHAPTER 16

THANK GOD FOR YOUR STORY: DELIVERANCE FROM BAD CHOICES

> Some sat in darkness, in utter darkness, prisoners suffering in iron chains, because they rebelled against God's commands and despised the plans of the Most High. So he subjected them to bitter labor; they stumbled, and there was no one to help. (Psalm 107:10–12 NIV)

God has a plan for our lives. Some of us have worried about discovering God's will for our lives to the point of being neurotic. Others of us do whatever we can to avoid doing what we know our Heavenly Father wants for us. Either way, we find ourselves fighting battles we cannot win.

This next story is about a group of people in need of rescue and who deliberately chose to disobey God. They were "rebels without a clue"! They had no idea where their choices are about to take them. The unknown poet expressed it this way:

Sin will take you further than you want to go.

Sin will keep you longer than you want to stay.

Sin will cost you more than you want to pay.

Two words are used to describe their choices: they rebelled and they despised. The word *rebel* carries the meaning of "bitterness" or "anger." A rebel attitude usually comes with the perception that "God is holding back from us something we want, so we will do it anyway." To despise is to reject with contempt what God means for our good.

First, let's clear up a misconception. We make bad choices, not mistakes. If I do something wrong and say, "Hey, guys, I just made a mistake!" I am trying to minimize my action. But if I say, "I made a bad choice," I am accepting full responsibility for my behavior.

I think this attitude of bitterness and contempt was the basis of the serpent's approach to Eve: "'You will not certainly die,' the serpent said to the woman. 'For God knows that when you eat from it your eyes will be opened, and you will be like God, knowing good and evil.' When the woman saw that the fruit of the tree was good for food and pleasing to the eye, and also desirable for gaining wisdom, she took some and ate it. She also gave some to her husband, who was with her, and he ate it" (Genesis 3:4–6 NIV).

Eve found the fruit to look very appealing. Then there was the thought, "We can be wise like God." Was the thought like, "God's keeping this wisdom from us. It's not fair"? She was fooled by the serpent. Adam witnessed this temptation, he knew exactly how it all went down and he knowingly ate the fruit. Bad choice. A very bad choice we all live with today.

In Psalm 107, the ones making bad decisions were a lot like people today—at least I know I am. I know it's wrong, but it just seems like the pleasure of my disobedience will be worth it. Something begins to happen as behaviors become habits and habits become addictions. The pleasure factor becomes less effective, less enjoyable. Life loses its luster. "Some sat in darkness, in utter darkness, prisoners suffering in iron chains" (verse 10).

"So he subjected them to bitter labor; they stumbled, and there was no one to help" (verse 12). I won't pretend to know what is going on in people's hearts. I do know my story and that of a select few who have taken me into their confidence. You know that guy who seems to be the envy of all the rest of the men in the office? You know, the ladies' man. He seems to have it all together. At the sales conferences, he gets the pretty girl every time.

But he's empty inside. He wants to stop the partying, the boozing, the women. He sleeps with women he doesn't even like because he can't say no. He would love to have a wife to be faithful to. He is miserable. He can't stop his carousing. He knows he is incapable of being faithful. He is tormented in the bondage of darkness created by his own bad choices. How do I know this is true? Hmm!

Empty, we live in darkness, bound in chains of slavery to sin. What do we do when we can't see our way out? First, let me say, a person, male or female, must be convinced that their bad choices are wrong before anything will ever change.

"Then they cried to the Lord in their trouble, and he saved them from their distress. He brought them out of darkness, the utter darkness, and broke away their chains" (107:13–14 NIV).

Again, help is as near as the cry of our heart. We have all prayed for divine rescue many times without success. What is the difference between our pleading for deliverance and the simple cry that rescues us from ourselves?

Let me pose this question in a little different context: We have a friend who is struggling to find salvation. They pray for forgiveness often. They serve tirelessly to help people. They attend church, but when asked, "Do you have a home in heaven?" Their best answer is, "Oh, I hope so!" But, they have no rest. What should we tell this friend to bring them peace with God?

Our friend is faced with the same conflict we are when we walk in the darkness of our rebellion. We are dealing with a faith crisis. We might tell our insecure friend, "God says it is impossible for him to lie. That means when he makes us a promise, he will absolutely keep it. He promised 'whoever calls on the name of the Lord shall be saved.' Do you believe that if you ask him right now to save you that would do it?"

I will admit to you my battles against my fleshly sin nature have not disappeared. I am still tempted and I do fail on occasions. The difference now is the iron shackles are broken. I am not bound in chains of slavery any more. When I fall, I know I am forgiven and I am empowered by my God to not wallow in my sin.

It is an issue of faith. Do you believe? Sometimes we hit rock bottom before we will give up our struggle and trust God fully. The choice is ours to rebel. The choice is ours to believe, to accept his rescue.

"Let them give thanks to the Lord for his unfailing love and his wonderful deeds for mankind, for he breaks down gates of bronze and cuts through bars of iron" (107:15–16 NIV).

Thanksgiving is a key to deliverance. Thanksgiving is an expression of faith. In my life, I can recognize times when giving of thanks came because of God's working. There have also been times of giving thanks before the answer is realized simply because I believe that what he has promised he will do.

Choices… choices! Will we make good choices, or will we make bad ones? Choose to believe his promises!

Listen to the promise God gave to Israel while they were enslaved to a Gentile country because of their rebel- lion: "Then you will call, and the Lord will answer; you will cry for help, and he will say: Here am I" (Isaiah 58:9 NIV).

CHAPTER 17

THANK GOD FOR YOUR STORY: THE SONG OF THE REDEEMED

You might be familiar with the fact that a psalm is a song; more particularly, it is a song of worship. In our study of Psalm 107, we are learning that it is a worship song of praise or thanksgiving for God's deliverance of the redeemed from our distresses.

In the first thirty-two verses, on five separate occasions, God's redeemed ones are implored to give thanks for his unfailing love, his goodness, and his wonderful works for us. Verse 1 seems to summarize these expressions: "Give thanks to the Lord, for he is good; his love endures forever" (NIV).

The simplest meaning for the word, thanks, in Hebrew, is "to lift the hands in worship." I was raised in a hand-raising church; and even now, I often see folks worship with hand gestures. A single raised hand seems to mean, "I identify with this message in song. It's me, Lord! You are talking to me!"

Sometimes I find myself spreading my arms open about waist-high. In my heart, I'm saying, "Fill me, Savior! I am open to you!" But raising both hands is an acknowledgement of thanks in which I am saying, "My Lord, my God! I lift my thanks to You! You are good! Your love never fails!"

We first learned about those wandering in desert wastelands (verses 4–9). They could not find their way home. Every night their hearts broke because they could not see even the glow of the lights of a distant city. Every day brought the disappointment of endless sand.

These sad, depressed people cried out in faith to the Lord, and he brought them to the city they longed for. And they gave thanks. They lifted their hands in praise (KJV) and, with full hearts, sang their thanks to their God who loves them unconditionally (unfailing) and poured out his goodness on them!

I have been there! It makes me want to dance with my hands raised high. "Thank You, Jesus! Thank You, Jesus!" The second group was bitter and angry (verses 10–16). They felt God was holding out on them. They disobeyed him. They didn't have a clue that the consequences of their choices would bind them in the blackest darkness of slavery. They found that doing what God prohibited led to misery.

But they, too, cried out to God in faith, and he rescued them out of their darkness, bondage, and misery. Something unusual happened the day that my cries were coupled with faith. Learning that he loved me unconditionally, despite my behavior, believing it, and understanding that our God never lies—these led me to trust him for a deliverance that was real.

So here we are together. We raise our hands in praise! Our hearts overflow with his unfailing love. Our souls are bathed in his wonderful works for all mankind. He rescued us! He loves us! He has always loved us. He shows his goodness all the time. Hallelujah!

In verses 17–22, we find a group I think all of us can identify with. These are called fools because of the rebellious choices they made. In contrast to the rebellion of verse 11 that was rooted in bitterness, they simply followed the inclination of their sinful nature. Me too.

The result was "affliction." "Some became fools through their rebellious ways and suffered affliction because of their iniquities" (verse 17 NIV). *Affliction*'s root meaning is "to be bowed down." I have the memory of carrying heavy sacks of cattle feed for long distances. When I could finally put the burden down, my shoulders felt light and weightless.

In this psalm, we learn that we are responsible for becoming fools by simply living life in our natural human way. The result is reaping the consequences of our actions. Paul warned us, "Do not be deceived: God cannot be mocked. A man reaps what he sows. Whoever sows to please their flesh, from the flesh will reap destruction; whoever sows to please the Spirit, from the Spirit will reap eternal life" (Galatians 6:7–8 NIV).

Reaping isn't much fun. We can reach the point when we wish it would end, but things we do can't be undone. Consequence lingers longer than we think they should, but we serve the God who "works for the good of those who love him" (Romans 8:28 NIV). It never ceases to amaze me how God has taken my bad choices and turned them into life- changing events for which I had longed. My years of pain are well worth the joy I am experiencing today.

We cry out in faith. He answers. "Then they cried to the Lord in their trouble, and he saved them from their distress. He sent out his word and healed them; he rescued them from the grave" (verses 1–20 NIV). Did you catch that? There is healing in his word. Sometimes consequences can't go away, but he can heal them into something good.

I've mentioned before about being diagnosed with bipolar disorder. I made bad choices during my unmanaged periods that cost me my ministry, my home, my wife, and, for a while, my children. God brought healing to my relationship with my children. The rest is gone forever. But! I am experiencing his unconditional love, the blessings of his wonderful goodness, and I am *happy*!

So, I lift my hands high! I raise my thanks to Jesus. I praise my God! Even though I have been oh so foolish, he has redeemed me! He showers me with his unfailing love! His goodness is to me, his own child!

CHAPTER 18

THANK GOD FOR YOUR STORY: WHEN LIFE HAPPENS

Well, tomorrow is the big day. Huge day—for me! Colonoscopy day! Yuck! So, that makes today preparation day. I'm sitting back in my recliner, shivering, hungry, waiting for the laxatives (plural) to do their job. I worked out in the garage until fatigue from the lack of food said, sitting down was a better option.

This isn't my first rodeo. This is probably the fourth or fifth time in the last decade. Persistent digestive problems have my specialists baffled, so they keep wanting to investigate what things look like on the inside. Every other time, the answer has been, "We didn't find anything, you hypochondriac!"

I'm sure you have noticed, while we are living, life happens. Our journeys are interrupted by unexpected events, surprises. Sometimes we feel like someone just gave us a hard punch in the gut. (Pun purely intentional).

Psalm 107:23–32 shares how life caught some sailors off guard. Verses 23–24: "Some went out on the sea in ships; they were merchants on the mighty waters. They saw the works of the Lord, his wonderful deeds in the deep" (NIV). Seasoned seamen sailed to trade their merchandise with buyers and sellers. As they made their way, favorable winds allowed them to observe the beauty and majesty of our Creator.

Smooth sailing! That is what we call it. We are just travelling along minding our own business, and things are good for a while. Maybe we are like those sailors; we witness his wondrous works around us. The giving of thanks comes easy.

But things can become complicated fast enough to make our heads spin. Verses 25–27: "For he spoke and stirred up a tempest that lifted high the waves. They mounted up to the heavens and went down to the depths; in their peril their courage melted away. They reeled and staggered like drunkards; they were at their wits' end" (NIV).

Have you ever been in open water when a storm blew in? My experience is minor compared to the storm that tossed this merchant ship. My wife, three young sons, and I were in my dad's small bass boat just enjoying a hot day cruising around a moderate-size state park lake.

When we saw a thunderstorm on the horizon, I turned the boat around and headed back to the docks. With no place to beach the boat and the boat floundering, we were close to panic. This is my family! The burden of responsibility lay heavy on my shoulders.

The experience of the sailors in Psalm 107 was very similar to ours. The boat's draft is very shallow. The waves tossed us up and down and side to side. I could see fear in the eyes of my wife and children. If we could have stood, I am sure we too would have staggered "like a drunk man." For a moment, my "wit's end" was about to unravel.

Isn't that what happens in life? We did nothing wrong to cause us to be caught in that storm. You did nothing wrong, but life has thrown its worst at you. Sicknesses come. Accidents happen. They are nobody's fault, but they are very real.

It does no good to ask, "Why?" My house burned down! The tornado destroyed my place of employment. My car broke down, and I can't get to work. My baby's sick. The list goes on, and the question still sweeps through our mind, "Why? What did I do to deserve this?"

We live in a fallen world. When Adam and Eve were exiled from the Garden of Eden, things started to go wrong. Paradise on earth is gone. Life happens. Life goes on. If you want to blame someone, blame Adam—but don't forget: given the same circumstances, you and I would have done the same thing.

There is hope. Psalm 107:28–30: "Then they cried out to the Lord in their trouble, and he brought them out of their distress. He stilled the storm to a whisper; the waves of the sea were hushed. They were glad when it grew calm, and he guided them to their desired haven." They were glad! Well, I guess so!

God answered their cries. He calmed the tempest. He stilled the storm to a whisper. It sounds a lot like a boat carrying the Son of God over the Sea of Galilee when a storm threatened to swamp the small craft. He calmed the seas with the simple words, "Peace, be still" (Mark 4:39, KJV). Both the disciples and those on the merchant ship were glad, and God brought them to their destination.

Sometimes we cry out, and God calms the storm; and other times, he calms our hearts. As I piloted my dad's small craft loaded with my family, I am sure we all prayed. The storm raged on, but a very peaceful calmness fell over me. I instructed my wife and sons to move to the front of the boat. The floundering boat planed out as I increased to full throttle. We rode on top of the waves for nearly a mile until we reached the harbor where the docks were located. To say we were "glad" is an understatement.

Whether God delivers us from the storm or through the storm, we can lift our hands in thanksgiving to our awesome Lord. "Let them give thanks to the Lord for his unfailing love and his wonderful deeds for mankind. Let them exalt him in the assembly of the people and praise him in the council of the elders" (107:31–32 NIV).

Tomorrow, my empty digestive track will be assaulted by sending a tube with a camera down my throat to take pictures of my stomach. Then my lower orifice will be violated by a different (I hope!) probe on an information-gathering expedition. Why? Because life happens. What if the news isn't good? Hey, this body is not designed to live forever. It will eventually wear out. Life happens.

Praise our Awesome God for his never-failing love and his great goodness to us all! There have been an untold number of storms we each have weathered. He has brought us through them all! We have stories to tell about how God held our hands through them all. I find these words of a popular gospel song from the 1970s to be a special blessing.

Andre Crouch with Bill and Gloria Gaither wrote the beautiful song, "Through It All." Their last verse is very thought provoking when "life happens."

> I thank God for the mountains,
> And I thank Him for the valleys,
> I thank Him for the storms
> He brought me through;
> For if I'd never had a problem
> I wouldn't know that He could solve them,
> I'd never know what faith in God could do.

By the way, if your doctor says something about a colonoscopy in your presence, don't volunteer!

PART 4

FINDING FAITH TO FORGIVE

CHAPTER 19

FORGIVENESS: AN IMPOSSIBLE TASK

Forgiveness. We can discuss with great joy the wondrous, amazing grace of our God who has forgiven us all our sins. Our hearts are thrilled by sermons, classes, and even one- on-one discussions about knowing we are forgiven!

Forgiveness. Nothing can quite compare to the discomfort we feel when we must extend it to another person who wronged us—especially when that person is unrepentant. Really, not only are they oblivious to our pain, they couldn't care less if we forgave them. Some people go so far as to try to convince us that we are the ones at fault. Why bother? They do not deserve our forgiveness!

A grandmother met her Sunday school teacher after a class that discussed forgiving others. She admitted her anger, bitterness, and complete unwillingness to forgive her son-in-law who molested his own daughters. Tears rolled down her cheeks as she shared her story.

A mother stood steadfastly with her daughter who accused her stepfather of groping her. As the mother refused to believe her husband's pleas of innocence, her face was literally "set like flint" against him. For reasons I do not understand, I said, "Let me take a guess. Something like this happened to you as a girl.

You told, but no one believed you. You swore to yourself if one of your daughters ever told you something like this, you would believe them." Almost imperceptibly, she nodded her head as tears streamed down her face.

Another mother found it extremely difficult to forgive the man who struck her son head-on as he rode his motorcycle. He was a newlywed and highly respected Christian man whose life was tragically cut short. Two hours after he crossed the double yellow line, the drunk driver's blood alcohol level was still two and a half times the legal limit.

Need I go on? Countless stories of betrayal, infidelity, lies, vindictiveness, gossip, slander, and much more could be said. Each time we think of our own personal circumstances, that ugly pain rears its vicious head and sears our hearts once again with flaming agony. We hurt so bad, we admit we just cannot forgive that person. Truth be told, we do not want to forgive.

What happens to us, in us, when all this turmoil is surging and abating in our souls? Some days are just worse than others. Maybe we feel like we have a grip on things, but if we are honest, we know what's going on beneath the surface when little things cause us to react far out of proportion to the current circumstances.

I will freely admit people sometimes do the most despicable acts against God's children, even when they claim to be one themselves. I do know that some things are so horrible, we find forgiveness is beyond our human ability.

My story of forgiveness is quite different. There have been people who have caused great pain to me, yet, my story of needing to forgive sounds almost like blasphemy. You see, I was angry with God! How could he let those things happen? Why did he make me that way? I prayed so hard, why didn't he answer? Why didn't he stop me?

Of course, my bitterness against God caused much deeper problems. With such feelings storming inside me, how could I have the strength to walk with him? My life spiraled out of control at an ever-increasing rate. My mental state deteriorated, and my behavior became irrational. As I sought to soothe my pain, I cut deeply into the hearts of those who loved me most.

With an ugly, bitter anger with God, especially for the pain I caused others, I told myself I hated everyone, especially myself. With such self-hatred, I believed all those who loved me were better off without me. I could not forgive myself. Tragically, I fell into a mental black hole. The only thought that could escape was I must either live with the terrible pain or die. So, I tried to die. Several times.

In this introduction to forgiveness, I am hoping we all can identify with the struggle to forgive. For some of us, extending forgiveness is the most difficult thing we will ever do. But when we think forgiving others is impossible, please realize it is not nearly as difficult as the alternative.

Let's visit the Sermon on the Mount when Jesus taught the multitudes what we call "The Lord's Prayer." In that prayer, which many of us repeat every week in church, we are taught to pray, "And forgive us our debts, as we forgive our debtors." (Matthew 6:12 KJV),

After finishing the prayer, Jesus explained himself, "For if you forgive other people when they sin against you, your heavenly Father will also forgive you. But if you do not forgive others their sins, your Father will not forgive your sins" (Matthew 6:14–15 NIV). I think it is interesting that this is the only part of the prayer that Jesus expanded upon. Perhaps this draws our attention to the potential our attitudes to others affect our relationship with God.

Frankly, I wish he had just left this part out of that beautiful prayer. But to add insult to injury, his disciples asked him to teach them to pray, and he repeated this part with only slightly different wording: "Forgive us our sins, for we also forgive everyone who sins against us" (Luke 11:4 NIV).

I don't think Jesus is saying that the Father breaks fellowship with us, but rather, the attitude of our heart is breaking our fellowship with him. You see, it isn't his fault, it is our decision that creates the conflict. Is it any wonder the commands of our Lord are to love our God, to love our neighbor, to love our enemies, and to love one another? (Matthew 22:37–39, 5:44; John 13:34).

If there were no other consequence of withholding forgiveness, this estrangement from God is the most immediate and probably the easiest for us to ignore. We feel distant from him. Prayer loses its priority in our spiritual lives. His word seems silent and difficult to understand. As the alienation continues, the pastor's sermons seem dry and irrelevant. It's tough getting out of bed and go to church. Why bother?

So why forgive? The consequences of not forgiving are way too expensive, and this is only the beginning.

CHAPTER 20

THE KING, DEBT, AND FORGIVENESS

Okay, we recognize that Jesus taught us to forgive others. If we refuse, there is the consequence of having a strained relationship with our Heavenly Father. So, what does it mean to *forgive*? Maybe there is some kind of loophole that will allow us to continue without messing around with our emotions. I just want to be mad!

I do know one thing it doesn't mean. Forgiving others does not mean we trust that person again. Trust must be earned. It can be lost in a moment's betrayal and cause suspicion to linger for years after forgiveness is granted. At times, an offending person may beg for our forgiveness, and we do. Yet we may never have a closeness to them again because there are consequences to those painful actions.

Another thing forgiveness may not necessarily mean is reconciliation. Reconciliation occurs when two or more parties are restored to a right or harmonious relationship with one another. However, sometimes restoration is impossible. If the person you are to forgive doesn't want to reconcile, there is nothing that can be done. Sometimes an offender has died, but we are still being victimized by their behavior toward us. Reconciliation is not possible, but forgiveness is.

Peter was curious about the subject of forgiveness, too, so he asks for us (because we really want to know this), "How many times do we forgive? Is seven times enough? That's an awful lot, you know! The rabbis teach us that three times is enough." Jesus tells us seven times doesn't even scratch the surface (Matthew 18:21–22). Forgiveness is unlimited. Then, as it was Jesus's custom, he tells us a story.

> Therefore, the kingdom of heaven is like a king who wanted to settle accounts with his servants. As he began the settlement, a man who owed him ten thousand bags of gold was brought to him. Since he was not able to pay, the master ordered that he and his wife and his children and all that he had be sold to repay the debt.
>
> At this the servant fell on his knees before him. "Be patient with me," he begged, "and I will pay back everything." The servant's master took pity on him, canceled the debt and let him go.
>
> But when that servant went out, he found one of his fellow servants who owed him a hundred silver coins. He grabbed him and began to choke him. "Pay back what you owe me!" he demanded.
>
> His fellow servant fell to his knees and begged him, "Be patient with me, and I will pay it back."
>
> But he refused. Instead, he went off and had the man thrown into prison until he could pay the debt. When the other servants saw what had happened, they were outraged and went and told their master everything that had happened.

> Then the master called the servant in. "You wicked servant," he said, "I canceled all that debt of yours because you begged me to. Shouldn't you have had mercy on your fellow servant just as I had on you?" In anger his master handed him over to the jailers to be tortured, until he should pay back all he owed.
>
> This is how my heavenly Father will treat each of you unless you forgive your brother or sister from your heart. (Matthew 18:23–35 NIV)

Jesus tells this story about a king whose servant owed him a significant unpayable debt: ten thousand bags of gold. In like manner, this bankrupt businessman had a friend who owed him a relatively small amount. If I may, I'll state the obvious. This is a tale about debt.

This goes well with the Lord's Prayer: "Forgive us our debts, as we also have forgiven our debtors" (Matthew 6:12 NIV). Forgiveness concerns a debt that is owed either to our God or to us from another. A debt is an obligation we owe to another.

But when Jesus amplified his teaching, he called that debt "sin" (NIV) or "trespasses" (KJV). To trespass means to step away from what is right and cross the line to do what is wrong. It is not a mistake (though we do make them) but a bad choice. In Luke 11:4, Jesus used a more general word for *sin, but* also the word we find in Matthew as *debt.*

No matter how you explain it, we are bankrupt before God because of our sins. At times, our fellow man will cross lines and be indebted to us. I don't think I've ever thought about the consequences of my actions quite that way until seeing it in these scriptures. I sinned against my wife, children, family, church, and everyone who ever trusted me. And yet I blamed God for it all. I crossed all kinds of lines. It was truly a huge, unpayable debt not only against people, but against our God as well.

Now Jesus tells us to forgive. The king forgave the servant an enormous debt, and that man's fellow servant asked only for time to pay. But the stinging rebuke is not that the servant did not give time for repayment, but that having been forgiven his bankruptcy as if he never incurred it, he refused to forgive his fellow servant the paltry sum.

There are two words in the New Testament translated "forgive." Jesus uses this one in every occurrence of forgiveness except one. On the other hand, Paul uses the other word every time, except once. The word Jesus favored basically means "to send away." We say things just a little differently today. We say, "Let go of it."

Someone is indebted to me. They sinned against me. What am I to do? Let it go! Oh man! That is such an oversimplification, it makes me nauseous! But does Jesus ever ask us to do anything he doesn't provide the means to accomplish? No!

For me, forgiveness is seldom a single act. It's more of a process, a step at a time. All I can do is to suggest you what has consistently worked for me.

First, I must acknowledge that I am obligated to God to forgive my offender. Why? Because he says I must if I want to get rid of the attitudes in me that poison my relationship with him.

Second, I confess my inability to forgive. I really need the Holy Spirit to strengthen me to let go of these nagging, harassing feelings.

Third, the process begins. Praying is a miracle method of producing forgiveness. It is helpful to me to pray, "Lord, with Your help and to the best of my ability, I forgive [name] for [offense]." Whenever the ugly feelings rear their heads, I repeat it. The first day, I may need to pray this way a hundred times, but tomorrow, it may only be ninety-nine times. Eventually, God will bring healing so that I remember the person apart from the feelings and maybe even apart from the debt.

Fourth, often release is possible by going to the person and confessing my negative feelings toward them and asking for their forgiveness. Airing dirty laundry, telling them just how I feel about the situation, seldom brings forgiveness or reconciliation. Assigning blame for the way I feel doesn't bring healing. Accepting my responsibility can bring honest forgiveness and hopefully reconciliation.

When the king confronted his unforgiving servant, after his judgment, he sentenced him to be tormented until the debt was paid. The epilogue, "This is how my heavenly Father will treat each of you unless you forgive your brother or sister from your heart" (Matthew 18:35 NIV).

We have already learned that withholding forgiveness creates in us an attitude that hinders our fellowship with God. But "tormentors"? What is Jesus telling us?

CHAPTER 21

THE GIFT OF FORGIVENESS

Sometimes I feel like I want to give another person a piece of my mind! Then I realize I can't afford to lose any more of what I have! Sometimes biting my tongue is the most difficult thing I must do.

My wife is a very kind, loving person, but it hasn't always been that way. As she has grown in her walk with Jesus, he has brought great change to her heart. She often laughs and says she was brought up in a home where "he who yells loudest, wins!"

A while back, she was involved in a casual conversation with another person when the subject of one of her children came up. This person shared some painful, malicious gossip that hurt deeply. How do you respond when someone verbally attacks your child, even though they are an adult?

God's grace was so evident and powerful in my wife's response. She said simply, "I don't even know how to respond to that." That was the end of that part of the conversation. Her answer did not end the relationship, but it did put an end to the gossip.

Forgiveness is so hard. Letting go is so hard. We fight the feeling of not wanting to forgive. We find ourselves thinking, *I'll never forgive [name] for [offense] as long as I live!* We honestly believe that the person does not deserve our forgiveness. And we are right. They don't deserve it, but neither do we.

But if we continue, according to our natural human inclinations, what happens? What about those tormentors Jesus warned about?

Remember, Jesus told us that withholding forgiveness hindered our relationship with God. King David wrote, "If I had cherished sin in my heart, the Lord would not have listened" (Psalm 66:18 NIV). Cherishing and nurturing our wounded heart result in a broken prayer life.

Don't get me wrong. We do need time to heal, but when the tormentors come and God seems absent, we should consider that perhaps it is time to let it go. In some cases, grief lasts a lifetime, but God loves us too much to want us to live with a life of withdrawal from him.

In his letter to the church in Ephesus, the apostle Paul reminded those early Christians what their life was like before they came into a relationship with Christ. I suppose it was no surprise to him that we carry baggage into our new life, for it is very apparent that Paul recognized that being a Christian does not eliminate problems with people.

> Do not let any unwholesome talk come out of your mouths, but only what is helpful for building others up according to their needs, that it may benefit those who listen. And do not grieve the Holy Spirit of God, with whom you were sealed for the day of redemption. Get rid of all bitterness, rage and anger, brawling and slander, along with every form of malice. Be kind and compassionate to one another, for- giving each other, just as in Christ God forgave you. (Ephesians 4:29–32 NIV)

Our words can have a positive or negative effect to those with whom we converse. Paul tells us not to tear down others with our words, but instead we should engage ourselves in talk that builds others up. He appeals for us to be perceptive of each other's needs. Otherwise, we grieve the Holy Spirit.

Think about tormentors for a moment. Consider the sadness we cause the Holy Spirit of God when we allow mean-spirited words to roll from our mouths toward others. I don't suppose I am the only person who speaks unwholesome (bad, rotten, or contemptuous) words to or about someone who has hurt me. However, I might be the king of contempt!

With the Holy Spirit grieved, the tormentors multiply. And here is the rub: It is our responsibility to rid the torturers from our lives. "Get rid of all bitterness, rage and anger, brawling and slander, along with every form of malice" (Ephesians 4:31–32 NIV).

I know what bitterness is. When the thought of a person or event passes in my mind, I speak bitter biting words expressing my hatefulness. To me, it feels like a dark cloud has fallen over my mind. I have left people, even my wife, speechless and dumbfounded.

Rage is the outward expression of my internal anger. When anger boils over, expressions of fury flow out of me. Generally speaking, people cannot conceive of me fuming out of control. But yes, it has happened. Brawling is violent behavior that can spill out of our souls. What? Have you never thrown anything or deliberately broke something handy or stomped out of the room?

Slander includes the unkind things we say. They are often untrue. We later admit we didn't mean what we said. Malice is the desire to hurt the other person back. We plan what we could say or wish we had thought to react in a more vicious way. Our minds are occupied with obsessive musings that replay the scenarios repeatedly underneath our fuming breath.

Earlier in Ephesians 4, Paul admitted that all anger is not wrong. "'In your anger do not sin': Do not let the sun go down while you are still angry, and do not give the devil a foothold" (verses 26–27). He tells us to admit we are angry, keep it temporary, and don't give the tormentor, Satan, a place for control in our lives.

But we are hurting! What do you expect us to do? Let's let God answer that question. "Be kind and compassionate to one another, forgiving each other, just as in Christ God forgave you" (Ephesians 4:32 NIV). Kindness, compassion, forgiveness.

The word for *forgiveness* Jesus used means "to let go." The word Paul used comes from the word normally translated as "grace." We remember in Ephesians 2:8–9, "For it is by grace you have been saved, through faith—and this is not from yourselves, it is the gift of God—not by works, so that no one can boast" (NIV).

Paul says we are saved by grace, and then he defined *grace* for us. Salvation is the gift of God. We cannot earn it or deserve it. Like the unmerciful servant in Jesus's story in Matthew 18 (see the last chapter: The King, Debt, and Forgiveness, we owed a debt of sin we could not pay. There could be no hope for us if our King does not suffer the loss of our bankruptcy by paying it himself. And he did. He let it go. He forgave our debt.

Paul described it as "grace," the gift of forgiveness: "Just as in Christ God forgave (graced) you." Do we deserve this grace, this forgiveness? No! Remember, "it is not by works, so that no one can boast." We do not deserve the gift of God's grace in forgiving us all our sins, but our loving God delighted to do it for us (John 3:16).

How are we to let go of the wrongs and hurt laden on us at the hands of other people? Grace. No, they do not deserve it, no more than we deserve to have our God's forgiveness. Our debt to him is insurmountably more than what anyone could owe us.

Let's set our goal to be kind and compassionate to others, even the ones who need our grace. So "let it go" and give an undeserved gift. Forgive. Even if they don't want it. The grace we give will free us from our tormentors.

CHAPTER 22

FORGIVENESS: LOOPHOLES OR HEALING?

Sometimes in the Bible, we find portions that seem to be exceptions to the rule. We find passages that clearly teach us how we ought to direct our lives. We may not particularly like the instructions, but we realize God's will is clear. Then we find another passage that seems to add a thought that appears to let us off the hook if we react in a different way.

I call this a loophole. Probably we are familiar with loopholes in our tax codes. We are especially irritated when we learn that the wealthy pay less taxes because something in the tax code in the form of tax shelters, deductions, or exclusion allows them to claim less income. We could do the same, but we don't have the income to meet the standards.

Some find a loophole for the Lord Jesus's command to forgive those who have hurt us in Luke 17:3–4, "If your brother or sister sins against you, rebuke them; and if they repent, forgive them. Even if they sin against you seven times in a day and seven times come back to you saying 'I repent,' you must forgive them" (NIV).

A man we'll call Dick and his fiancé sat in a Sunday school class I was in as we discussed forgiveness. His divorce had been messy and painful. His former wife had precipitated the breakup of the marriage by her infidelity. Their children were hurt deeply. I really do not know the specifics, only that she left behind the shattered lives of her family.

The wife was unrepentant. Dick had seemed to move ahead with his life and was anticipating being married soon. Still, since his ex was not sorry for her actions, he felt he was not obligated to forgive her. He believed the passage in Luke did indeed let him off the hook.

Really, giving a loophole was not the purpose of Jesus's lesson here. The point of this short sermon was the necessity of unlimited forgiveness. "The apostles said to the Lord, 'Increase our faith!'" (Luke 17:5 NIV). They were blown away by Jesus's assertion that forgiveness is unlimited. I mean seven times in one day! Think of it. It had to be deliberate! God knows *we* would never do something like that! Can you see their jaw dropped open in surprise?

Here is the real shocker. Jesus's response reveals that it is not so much a matter of faith as it is a matter of obedience. Faith is always important. We must have faith to be obedient. But it is not central here. Notice what Jesus said. "If you have faith as small as a mustard seed, you can say to this mulberry tree, 'Be uprooted and planted in the sea,' and it will obey you" (Luke 17:6 NIV). Faith, even in small amounts, accomplishes great things. But don't let your feelings of not having enough faith keep you from being obedient.

Jesus told a story to illustrate what he meant.

> Suppose one of you has a servant plowing or looking after the sheep. Will he say to the servant when he comes in from the field, "Come along now and sit down to eat"? Won't he rather say, "Prepare my supper, get yourself ready and wait on me while I eat and drink; after that you may eat and drink"? Will he thank the servant because he did what he was told to do? So,

> you also, when you have done everything you were told to do, should say, "We are unworthy servants; we have only done our duty" (Luke 17:7–10 NIV).

The servant did his job. He worked all day and came into the house. Instead of sitting down to a prepared meal as we might expect, he was told to prepare the master's supper. Then he sat down to eat, himself. Jesus asked if the servant would be thanked by his master. This is a rhetorical question. The answer is, "No!" Why? Because he was just doing his job. Honestly, I have been so seldom thanked for my work it was almost a shock when I was!

Jesus's application reveals that when we have obeyed and given unlimited forgiveness, recognize that we have only done what Jesus told us to do. When we forgive, we are doing what is right to do. However, as we have learned from our previous lessons, our unwillingness to forgive brings tormentors into our lives, which steals from us the joy of living.

There are psychologists and counselors who believe the refusal to forgive is the root of depression in many people. We can be totally robbed of our peace. We are not designed to carry around the burden of bitterness and anger.

What has forgiveness meant to me? I was angry with God and unable to forgive myself. There were people I needed to forgive, but I was being eaten alive by bitterness. It was like a cancer in my soul. In one word, forgiveness meant "healing."

I blamed God for making me the way I was, which caused me to do the things I did. He made me bipolar. He made me with my weaknesses. He allowed me to hurt my family. He didn't answer my prayers. He didn't deliver me from my addictions. I did not believe he loved me. I called myself an abused child of God, a pawn in a supernatural chess game.

Consequently, I hated myself. I had a suicidal hatred. A friend told me, "Charlie, you need to forgive yourself." Being the smart aleck that I am, I said, "Fine, I'll forgive myself. Tell me how!" Of course, there is no formula. What was I to do?

Truth began to dawn on my clouded mind as I progressed from bad to worse. I had to hit bottom before I found the only way to look was up. First, I came to realize my circumstances were not God's fault. I made my own decisions, so I alone was responsible for the consequences. God could have made me differently, but bipolar disorder is thought to be genetic in nature. He allows nature to take its own course. I am still "fearfully and wonderfully made" (Psalm 139:14).

This was a long process that I hope to share sometime in the future. Realizing God loved me, even though I had railed against him, brought a genuine peace. I imagined as I cursed him, He would smile and say, "My child, I love you!"

Experiencing his love, I repented of my sin and called on his name. I know he forgave me, because he said he would (1 John 1:9). With the realization of his love came the release of my self-hatred. Finally, I could forgive myself because of his great love for me. Peace, peace, blessed peace has flooded my soul.

I doubt that anyone can benefit from a loophole in forgiveness, but all benefit from his healing grace when we forgive. If anyone is hanging on to their pain, I imagine the day is soon coming when your weary soul will compel you to find relief. My prayer is that you will find his rest.

> Come to me, all you who are weary and burdened, and I will give you rest. Take my yoke upon you and learn from me, for I am gentle and humble in heart, and you will find rest for your souls. For my yoke is easy and my burden is light. (Matthew 11:28–30 NIV)

CHAPTER 23

THE FINE ART OF GETTING EVEN!

"I don't get mad! I get even!"

> "You know what they say about paybacks!" "Revenge is sweet!"

"I don't live by the golden rule. I live by the broken rule! If you break my rules, I'll break you in half! You know, an eye for an eye, a tooth for a tooth. Hey, it's biblical!"

How many hours have been wasted daydreaming about the best way to get back at the object of our anger? It's only human nature, and God knows our tendencies. It is normal to lash back immediately. Verbal altercations often erupt. We trade verbal punches, arguments designed to inflict pain on the other. We cannot hear what the other person is saying because we are too busy planning what we will say next. Nobody wins.

At times, we meet our antagonists with silence. Life goes on while we do a slow burn. In the meantime, as our lives continue, we are negatively impacted, and our hearts are heavy. We are not designed by our God to live day in and day out with such brokenness.

What are we to do with this drive to lash out, to harm, to pay back the one who has hurt us? We have learned in our previous studies forgiveness is possible. But we have that nagging thought in the back of our minds, "They shouldn't be allowed to get away with this! It's not fair!"

God has set up some scriptural laws that promise us how God deals with these problems in our lives. We can fully trust him in all matters in our lives, even when others hurt us. Nothing misses his attention.

The first scriptural principle is "*Revenge belongs to God.*" I never need to concern myself with exacting punishment on those who hurt me. Here is how the apostle Paul stated it, "Do not repay anyone evil for evil. Be careful to do what is right in the eyes of everyone. If it is possible, as far as it depends on you, live at peace with everyone. Do not take revenge, my dear friends, but leave room for God's wrath, for it is written: 'It is mine to avenge; I will repay,' says the Lord" (Romans 12:17–19 NIV).

What is our responsibility when we are wronged? Do right by doing everything possible to live at peace with everyone. Our testimony is at stake! Leave the whole matter in God's hands.

"Do not say, 'I'll pay you back for this wrong!' Wait for the Lord, and he will avenge you" (Proverbs 20:22 NIV). Think about this for a moment. No one can hurt any one of us and get away with it! Think about it! Anyone who hurts another must face God for what he has done, either in this world or in the world to come!

Yet God warns us not to rejoice when we see him bring his judgment. "Do not gloat when your enemy falls; when they stumble, do not let your heart rejoice, or the Lord will see and disapprove and turn his wrath away from them" (Proverbs 24:17–18 NIV). God is in the business of building people who do what is right. Rejoicing in the harm that comes to others is not a good thing to do.

In recognizing this truth as it applied to me, I became troubled that those who hurt me would give an account to God. I would personally rather the person get their heart right with God than face his vengeance; so, I pray for them. I'm no super saint. This is the burden God has placed on my heart. I do know of cases when I prayed for the offending person and still saw the vengeance God brought to them. It has brought no joy to my heart.

The second scriptural principle is "*We reap what we sow.*" "Do not be deceived: God cannot be mocked. A man reaps what he sows. Whoever sows to please their flesh, from the flesh will reap destruction; whoever sows to please the Spirit, from the Spirit will reap eternal life" (Galatians 6:7–9 NIV). Some call it karma. Those from my heritage say, "What goes around comes around."

A denominational church leader was moderating an all-church meeting in which a pastor was being torn to pieces by accusations that were damaging to him personally and destructive to his ministry in that church. The charges were being leveled by a much younger associate pastor. In the end, the church voted to oust their pastor of many years.

The moderator turned to the young associate and said, "Son, there will come a day when God will turn this back on your head." When the moderator and pastor returned home, the pastor broke into bitter crying and wailing. The church leader tried to comfort him, but the now former pastor said, "No, leave me alone!"

After some time, the pastor calmed down, and in a voice broken and barely audible, he said, "What that young man did to me tonight, I did to my pastor when I was his age. God has turned it back on my head."

The third scriptural principle is "God *never overlooks the good things we do.*" If we sow to the Spirit, we will reap spiritual benefits. "Let us not become weary in doing good, for at the proper time we will reap a harvest if we do not give up. Therefore, as we have opportunity, let us do good to all people, especially to those who belong to the family of believers" (Galatians 6:9–10 NIV).

If anyone deserved the right to exact revenge, that person would be Joyce Meyer. I invite you to read her story for yourself at www.joycemeyer.org. Her father was a verbally, emotionally, physically, and sexually abusive man. He ruled the home like a tyrant leaving all members of the household in fear. He began sexually abusing her as a young child and continued until she left the home at age eighteen.

To say that the abuse had a negative impact on her adult life would be the understatement of the century. Saved as a girl, she had a lot of growing to do, just as we all do. Slowly, she began to grow in Christ one issue at a time. She answered God's call to ministry while still dealing with her childhood trauma.

She finally surrendered her life to Christ and forgave her father for raping her over two hundred times. She forgave her mother who was aware of the abuse, but was too frightened of her husband to do anything about it. This was a miraculous working of God's grace in her heart.

But the story wasn't over. God wanted to do more. He spoke to Joyce's heart with the burden to care for her sick, elderly parents during their final years. As she obeyed, she had the privilege of leading both her mother and her father to faith in Jesus Christ. She was doing good to all, and God was honoring his Word.

Our God promised to take care of our past. He forgave all our sins. He promised to take care of our future and gave us eternal life. And now we learn he has promised to take care of our present. No one can harm us and get away with it. We can trust him completely.

PART 5

OUR SPIRITUAL DECLARATION OF INDEPENDENCE

CHAPTER 24

THE PERFORMANCE TRAP

There is a question that often nags in the minds of many hurting people: Do I really matter? It strikes at the heart of our insecurities and feelings of inferiority. Does God care about me when my circumstances challenge the very thought?

Twenty-first-century Americans are caught in a performance trap. To succeed, we must do. If we fail, we ask, "What more could I have done?" This even affects our relationships. Numerous times spouses have approached me with stories of mates who have withdrawn from them. Without fail, whenever I asked, "What can you do to make your husband/wife love you?" they were dumbfounded. There is nothing we can do! Nothing! We can't make another person do anything. But still, they were caught in the performance trap.

This is not so with our God. His love is unconditional and never-ending. There is nothing we can do to earn his love or to deserve it. Yet in our performance-driven society, we can get caught up in the deception that if we do enough, God will accept us.

For reasons that aren't all that important now, I felt totally unlovable to God and people. I thought, *if you really knew me, you wouldn't love me.* Maybe on the human level, it might be true, but I felt totally unlovable to God. That is, until one day, I stumbled on an old familiar verse I knew by heart. I saw it in an entirely new light.

"But God demonstrates his own love for us in this: While we were still sinners, Christ died for us" (Romans 5:8 NIV). Five undeniable truths unfolded out of this single verse.

FIRST, GOD LOVES ME JUST AS I AM

He loved us "while we were still sinners." While we were still unforgiven, in our worst possible condition, laden down with sin and on our way to a Christless eternity, he loved us. His love was so great Christ died for us to pay the penalty of our sins.

"But because of his great love for us, God, who is rich in mercy, made us alive with Christ even when we were dead in transgressions" (Ephesians 2:4, 5; NIV). "This is how God showed his love among us: He sent his one and only Son into the world that we might live through him" (1 John 4:9 NIV).

Perhaps the first Bible verse you ever learned was John 3:16, "For God so loved the world that he gave his one and only Son, that whoever believes in him shall not perish but have eternal life" (NIV). Maybe the first song you learned was "Jesus Loves Me." "Whoever" covers each of us no matter how unlovable and worthless we may perceive ourselves to be. I am so bold as to say to believe God does not love me is to believe a lie from the pit of hell!

SECOND, GOD DOES NOT HAVE FAVORITES

God has never loved anyone more than he loves me (or you)! This is so amazing! Yes, we are each individuals and God treats us as such. Some of us have very traumatic stories when we wonder where God was during that time. However, our circumstances do not alter God's promises. This idea of favorites is another aspect of the performance trap. It's the competitive energy that says "if only

I can change this part of me, God would give me good things, like 'Joe Christian' over there."

Here is what Scripture says about our God: "Jesus Christ is the same yesterday and today and forever" (Hebrews 3:8 NIV). "Every good and perfect gift is from above, coming down from the Father of the heavenly lights, who does not change like shifting shadows" (James 1:17 NIV).

Since he does not change, his attributes do not change. He loves me fully with all the love he has. Furthermore, God never has favorites: "For God does not show favoritism" (Romans 2:11 NIV).

THIRD, THERE IS NOTHING I CAN DO TO MAKE GOD LOVE ME MORE

In our performance-driven society, I have met genuine believers who were the most diligent workers in the church. In private conversation, some confessed feeling that if they could do just a bit more, they could believe God loved them. They found themselves on a vicious treadmill, trying to make themselves more lovable to God.

One dear lady was so beaten down by her past, she could not believe God loved her. Yet she loved him so much, she gave tireless service for his name's sake. I often told her, "Jesus loves you." Her answer, "That's what they say." After a few years, she finally responded, "Yes, he does!" Happy day! He loved us in our most despicable condition. He forgave our sins and made us his children. He never changes.

His love is unconditional.

FOURTHLY, THERE IS NOTHING I CAN DO TO MAKE HIM LOVE ME LESS

Before we could do anything good or bad, our God had already loved us to the point of sending his Son into this world to pay for our sins. Repeatedly, the Psalm writers proclaimed his love to be "unfailing." "I have always been mindful of your unfailing love and have lived in reliance on your faithfulness" (Psalm 26:3 NIV).

Perhaps you remember the story of the prodigal son. The story has more to do with the father than it does with the wayward son. The son wasted his life and squandered his father's fortune in a debased lifestyle. But as soon as the father saw him a great distance away, he ran to the son, fell on his neck, cried, and rejoiced: his son was home! That is how God loves us.

But, Charlie, you don't know what I've done! True. God does, and he pledged his unfailing love to you.

FIFTH, BECAUSE HE LOVE US, WE ARE THE WINNERS

It's all summed up in Romans 8:35–37, "Who shall separate us from the love of Christ? Shall trouble or hardship or persecution or famine or nakedness or danger or sword? As it is written: 'For your sake we face death all day long; we are considered as sheep to be slaughtered.' No, in all these things we are more than conquerors through him who loved us" (NIV).

More than "conquerors!" This is a superlative statement. A conqueror is one who wins a battle. But the battle was not won by the skin of our teeth. It was and is won through the decisive victory of Christ's blood and his resurrection from the dead. Paul writes, "'Where, O death, is your victory? Where, O death, is your sting?' The sting of death is sin, and the power of sin is the law.

But thanks be to God! He gives us the victory through our Lord Jesus Christ" (1 Corinthians 15:55–57 NIV).

Why don't you right now close your eyes and quietly hum, "Yes, Jesus loves me! Yes! Jesus loves me! Yes! Jesus loves me! The Bible tells me so!"

CHAPTER 25

FREE AT LAST! FREE AT LAST!

Some of us couldn't wait to leave home. When we hit that eighteenth birthday, we planned to move out and make our own way in the world. No more rules, no curfews, no nagging. We were so tired of being told what to do by our parents, school, coaches, and maybe even our church.

Little did we realize we were trading one set of rules for another. One young man recently thought he would escape the bondage of home by joining the Marines! I wonder what was going through his mind after that first week of boot camp?

For some folks, on the other hand, rules are comfortable. Our lives resemble chaos, and we seek rules to bring in a sense of order. I fit into a church background that gave rules to follow to be a spiritual Christian. If I could keep the rules, and conquer my physical appetites, then I would be a victorious Christian. Kind of makes sense, in a human manner of thinking, don't you think?

When one set of rules seemed to bring a measure of success, I would add more rules because there was still a void in my heart. Strange as it may sound, the better I did, the burden to be even better became heavier and more painful. I was more conscious of my failings. So, the list of rules grew.

I once said from the pulpit, "The closer I walk with Christ, the more I am aware of my sinfulness." I watched as I saw one man's head nod in sad agreement. There is a term for this. It is called legalism. How easy it had been to forget that Jesus died to set us free from the bondage of rules.

The fear of legalism for me was if I removed the rules, I automatically opened the door of license to sin. If there were no definitive list of do's and don'ts, I would by virtue of my sin nature choose to do wrong. I guess I believed a list of rules made it easier to do right. Really, that made spirituality an illusion.

As believers in Jesus Christ, we can be so busy serving Christ in our church and community that we might be compared to Martha, the sister of Mary and Lazarus. She had the opportunity of a lifetime. Imagine, fixing dinner for Jesus! I love to cook, so I can imagine her planning and preparation of the best lamb chops she had ever fixed!

She was super busy and needed some help in the kitchen, but Mary wasn't at all concerned. She sat at Jesus's feet listening to him teach. I think Martha was what we call "being a martyr" as she complained to Jesus. "But Martha was distracted by all the preparations that had to be made. She came to him and asked, "Lord, don't you care that my sister has left me to do the work by myself? Tell her to help me!" (Luke 10:40 NIV).

"Martha, Martha," the Lord answered, "you are worried and upset about many things, but few things are needed—or indeed only one. Mary has chosen what is better, and it will not be taken away from her" (verses 41–42 NIV).

Martha had the "*illusion of spirituality*" as she hastened about serving Jesus. It was part of her inner conviction that she must do her best for the Master! Yet she became frustrated and judgmental of her sister because Mary was not willing to get up and help her with her chores. Neither Martha's list of rules nor ours will make us into the servants of God with genuine spirituality.

The letters of Paul reveal that this issue of rules was an ever-present problem in the first-century church. There was a group of teachers who invaded the churches with the message that Gentiles had to become Jews and keep the law of Moses to be saved.

While this early church problem may not be as prevalent today, I still find many believers struggling in their spiritual lives to find the balance freedom in Christ brings to us. Paul had a simple message for the early church and to us as well. The solution to subjection to rules is to conduct our lives by the Holy Spirit. Paul's letter to the Galatians could be called the Christian Declaration of Independence.

> It is for freedom that Christ has set us free. Stand firm, then, and do not let yourselves be burdened again by a yoke of slavery… You, my brothers and sisters, were called to be free. But do not use your freedom to indulge the flesh; rather, serve one another humbly in love. For the entire law is fulfilled in keeping this one command: "Love your neighbor as yourself." (5:1, 13, 14; NIV).

Paul used the whole book to expound on our freedom in Christ. When he comes to chapter 5, he teaches us the alternative to living by the rules is to be controlled by the Spirit by sharing the contrasts in our lives when we walk in the flesh and when we walk by the Holy Spirit.

I want to be honest. Not everyone who says they have a relationship with Christ, but really are not much concerned about pleasing God, will be interested in this subject. But if you care and you want a closeness with your Savior, I pray you will find the next few chapters to be life transforming.

CHAPTER 26

SIX HUNDRED-THIRTEEN RULES!

After reading the introductory article in this series, "A Spiritual Declaration of Independence," one reader responded, "This subject seems to be hard to understand. The Bible is full of rules. Like the Pharisee, we tend to add to the rules of do's and don'ts. So, what does it really mean to be free? It's kind of hard to shake a mentality of being judgmental and one of self-condemnation if you were indoctrinated that way."

These observations very aptly illustrate the struggle Christianity has faced from the beginning of the church, as we are learning from the Galatians. The early church fathers continued to seek a biblical understanding of true spiritual holiness.

Starting in about AD 250, monasteries began to rise, not only as learning centers, but also as homes for an ascetic or self-denial living. Hermits existed alone in wilderness places because they believed that depriving themselves of comforts and the presence of people would allow them to concentrate solely on their relationship with Christ with- out fleshly distractions. Their energies were used to concentrate on spiritual matters and holy living.

Through the centuries, the church has evolved in many different directions. We call them abominations (oops, denominations). Some of these differences revolve around the rules that the groups adhere to. For those of us concerned with holy living, we must deal with our humanity and our sin nature. The question arises, "How much sin is too much?" since we all admit that we do sin.

Before we deal with our Spiritual Declaration of Independence, maybe it would be helpful if we examine why the Bible is filled will all those rules. Scholars have counted 613 laws (absolute rules in the first five books of the OT (Old Testament) called collectively the Law. These were the regulations by which the people of God were to govern their lives.

The first thing we can learn from the Law is a description of what actions on our part are "sin." Paul explained it this way to the church in Rome, "What shall we say then? Is the Law sin? May it never be! On the contrary, I would not have come to know sin except through the Law; for I would not have known about coveting if the Law had not said, 'You shall not covet.' But sin, seizing the opportunity afforded by the commandment, produced in me every kind of coveting" (Romans 7:7–8 NIV).

Paul is teaching us that a major drawback of the Law is its tendency to provoke our sin nature. It's like telling a child watching a ball game, "You can stand by the bleachers, but don't cross the foul line." As you watch the child, sure enough, they look back into the stands and deliberately place one foot across the line to see what you will do. Yeah, I know, your little angels would never do such a thing but mine sure did!

Now we recognize exactly by our knowing God's law what sin is, that is, which actions or attitudes are displeasing to him. Through the Law, we learn the NT (New Testament) truth that "the wages of sin is death" (Romans 6:23 NIV). If God's people broke the rules, God provided a sufficient animal sacrifice to die in place of the offender. Therefore, we learn just how serious sin really is. If a person sinned, his punishment was death unless a suitable substitute was found to die in his stead.

I realize the OT depicts God's hatred for sin, and his anger toward those who commit sin is clearly revealed. We witness his judgment, not only against the pagans and theirpractices, butt against his people when they are unrepentant. Paul has something to tell us about this.

"Therefore the Law has become our tutor to lead us to Christ, so that we may be justified by faith. But now that faith has come, we are no longer under a tutor" (Galatians 3:24–25, NASB. The aim of the Law was to reveal our need of Christ. Remember, Jesus told us, "Do not think that I have come to abolish the Law or the Prophets; I have not come to abolish them but to fulfill them" (Matthew 5:17– 18 NIV).

All the righteous requirements of the Law were fulfilled in Christ's work in his death on the cross, his burial, and resurrection. Through his letters, Paul consistently reveals that salvation is a gift of God's grace through faith alone (see Ephesians 2:8-9). This gift is free for us, but the cost had to be paid by someone. That "Someone" was Jesus. The real shocker revealed in Galatians is we no longer need the Law after it has brought to Christ because the penalty for our sins is paid in full by Christ!

When we concentrate on rules, our flesh rebels against them, and we fall into the snare of sin. As we focus on rules, we find ourselves weakened as we yield. When our focus is on our weaknesses, we focus more on our rules. We use all our own strength to obey, but our strength is not enough. Again, listen to our struggle Paul shares with us.

> "For I know that good itself does not dwell in me, that is, in my sinful nature. For I have the desire to do what is good, but I cannot carry it out. For I do not

do the good I want to do, but the evil I do not want to do—this I keep on doing. Now if I do what I do not want to do, it is no longer I who do it, but it is sin living in me that does it. So, I find this law at work: Although I want to do good, evil is right there with me. For in my inner being I delight in God's law; but I see another law at work in me, waging war against the law of my mind and making me a prisoner of the law of sin at work within me. What a wretched man I am! Who will rescue me from this body that is subject to death? Thanks be to God, who delivers me through Jesus Christ our Lord!" (Romans 7:18–25 NIV).

What do we learn from God's list of rules?

1. We know what sin is. If we do not understand the seriousness of sin, how can we ever understand the wonder of the grace of God?
2. We know what the penalty of sin is. If we don't understand that sin has a consequence, how can we understand God's gift of eternal life?
3. We learn we are powerless over sin in our own strength. If we do not understand our powerlessness over sin, how could we understand the need for faith alone in the finished work of Christ? "Know that a person is not justified by the works of the law, but by faith in Jesus Christ. So, we, too, have put our faith in Christ Jesus that we may be justified by faith in Christ and not by the works of the law, because by the works of the law no one will be justified" (Galatians 2:16–17 NIV).
4. We learn that it is impossible for the Law to give life. It only brings death. Faith brings life. "For if a law had

been given that could impart life, then righteousness would certainly have come by the law. But Scripture has locked up everything under the control of sin, so that what was promised, being given through faith in Jesus Christ, might be given to those who believe" (Galatians 3:21–22 NIV).

CHAPTER 27

LAW? FREEDOM? I'M SO CONFUSED!

We live by rules. There were rules established by our parents. Most of them were beneficial to us, though, as we grew older, some no longer were needed. They were designed to teach us discipline, safety or respect. There were rules at school, and as adults, "policies" govern the workplace. My state has a big thick book—all in fine print, numbered with endless subsections—called *The Ohio Revised Code*, a fancy way of saying "state laws."

Frankly, we need all these different forms of rules because of our human nature. Laws allow us to live at peace with one another and establish boundaries within which we must live. These rules are much like the OT law. They are good, but with limitations.

The apostle Paul never discounts the necessity of the Law in our lives. Even in the middle of our Spiritual Declaration of Independence, he reveals law breaking as the opposite of the life that can be ours as we walk in the step with the Holy Spirit. There is an odd twist here we need to recognize. Keeping the law that governs our behavior does not make us spiritual or set us free. But breaking those laws does bind us in sin and interrupts our fellowship with God. Confused?

We have a choice to either walk according to our flesh (our old sin nature that is in conflict with the Spirit) or in the Spirit. If we are a Law breaker, we are living in submission to our sin nature. The real question that comes to my mind is, "How do I stop living as a Law breaker?" Answer: Live the way God has designed for us to live. Inside my mind, I want to scream, "How? Tell me the rules!" I'm so confused!

> So, say, walk by the Spirit, and you will not gratify the desires of the flesh. For the flesh desires what is contrary to the Spirit, and the Spirit what is contrary to the flesh. They are in conflict with each other, so that you are not to do whatever you want. But if you are led by the Spirit, you are not under the law. The acts of the flesh are obvious: sexual immorality, impurity and debauchery; idolatry and witchcraft; hatred, discord, jealousy, fits of rage, selfish ambition, dissensions, factions and envy; drunkenness, orgies, and the like. I warn you, as I did before, that those who live like this will not inherit the kingdom of God. (Galatians 5:16–21 NIV)

Obviously, a war exists between our sin nature (our natural sinful choices) and the Holy Spirit. It is also easy to see that the acts of the flesh are violations of God's Law. Paul unapologetically repeats similar lists in almost all his letters and calls them "sin" that should not be part of a Christian's life. So how can Paul say at the same time that we are free from the Law?

Confused? Instead of working through this seeming conflict, I defaulted to legalism. The rules were more comfortable than freedom. It allows us to sit in judgment, not only over our personal lives, but over the lives of others as well. We have just read one in the list of broken rules. We realize that knowing the rules does not empower us to conquer our sinful human nature. What can? Suddenly, the rules don't seem so comfortable anymore.

Paul addressed this apparent conflict between law and grace in Romans 5–8. "The law was brought in so that the trespass might increase. But where sin increased, grace increased all the more, so that, just as sin reigned in death, so also grace might reign through righteousness to bring eternal life through Jesus Christ our Lord" (Romans 5:20–21 NIV).

Grace! Wonderful *grace*! Grace conquers the sin nature demonstrated by the breaking of the rules. The more the law is broken, the more grace is revealed. So, we might say, "Wow, wonderful! I can live any way I want to! It doesn't matter because grace covers it all. If I sin, I'll confess it and go out and do it again!" I mean, really?

"What shall we say, then? Shall we go on sinning so that grace may increase? By no means! We are those who have died to sin; how can we live in it any longer?" (Romans 6:1–2 NIV). Get it? There is no license to sin. In Christ, we are dead to sin. Paul teaches that as lost people, we were slaves to our sin nature; but as believers, we are slaves to righteousness.

I am reminded of a true story a friend of mine told. He was working as an orderly in a hospital morgue. Part of his job was to prepare bodies for transport by the funeral homes. He was training a new young man on the procedures, and it was very apparent the new guy was uncomfortable and fearful to work with dead people.

My friend was teaching his new friend to lay one hand of the cadaver over the other and loosely tie them together. As he reached for the string, the hand on the bottom slipped loose and slid off the cart and banged loudly against the trays on the shelf below. The next thing he saw was the newbie trying to push open a pull only door!

Why? Because it is unnatural for dead people to move! Just as it is not normal for those who are dead to sin to continue living in the realm of sin. But… but… but. I don't feel dead. This is not something we are to feel, but it is what we are to believe.

> In the same way, count yourselves dead to sin but alive to God in Christ Jesus. Therefore, do not let sin reign in your mortal body so that you obey its evil desires. Do not offer any part of yourself to sin as an instrument of wickedness, but rather offer yourselves to God as those who have been brought from death to life; and offer every part of yourself to him as an instrument of righteousness. For sin shall no longer be your master, because you are not under the law, but under grace. (Romans 6:11–14 NIV)

We have a choice in the way we live. The best choice is not to be in subjection to rules, but to grace. This is a truth we must believe before grace will be effective in our lives. We must believe that we are dead to sin and alive to righteousness. What are our choices? Believe the truth or not. Remember, "without faith it is impossible to please God" (Hebrews 11:6 NIV). God doesn't give commands that he fails to provide to us the means of keeping them.

We saw in Romans 7 Paul had issues learning how to do live under grace because of the war between his sin nature and the Spirit (see "Six Hundred-Thirteen Rules!"). He knew he did not have a license to sin. He reasoned, legalism is the way to go. Keep the rules! But he failed. He cried out in his frustration, much like I have done, "What a wretched man I am! Who will rescue me from this body that is subject to death?" (7:24 NIV).

Thankfully, he gives us the answer, "Thanks be to God, who delivers me through Jesus Christ our Lord!" (7:25 NIV). Just two verses away, he draws this conclusion, "Therefore, there is now no condemnation for those who are in Christ Jesus, because through Christ Jesus the law of the Spirit who gives life has set you free from the law of sin and death" (8:1–2 NIV).

Before we can progress to learning how to live the way God has designed for us to live, these are truths we must believe first. In other words, we can't make this happen. If the great, godly apostle Paul could not achieve the goal of making himself obedient, how could I ever expect to do it? There is an answer. Paul called it "the law of the Spirit."

Stay tuned.

CHAPTER 28

A RULE WE CAN LIVE WITH

Okay, enough of the rules. It's all negative. If we are not to govern our lives by them, then it is time we learn about our independence. Freedom is our new birthright. It's time to emphasize the positive! "It is for freedom that Christ has set us free" (Galatians 5:1 NIV). This is who we are, believe it or not.

If it seems unreasonable to be able to live a godly life apart from the rules, God leaves us with a guide by which we can recognize what our lives should look like. "Let no debt remain outstanding, except the continuing debt to love one another, for whoever loves others has fulfilled the law. The commandments, 'You shall not commit adultery,' 'You shall not murder,' 'You shall not steal,' 'You shall not covet,' and whatever other command there may be, are summed up in this one command: 'Love your neighbor as yourself.' Love does no harm to a neighbor. Therefore, love is the fulfillment of the law" (Romans 13:8–10 NIV).

It should be no surprise Paul revealed this truth to us in Galatians after he taught us we are to live by faith and not by the rules. "For the entire law is fulfilled in keeping this one command: 'Love your neighbor as yourself.' If you bite and devour each other, watch out or you will be destroyed by each other" (Galatians 5:14–15 NIV). He then reveals the works of the flesh.

Loving one another means we are living out the golden rule Jesus gave us: "So in everything, do to others what you would have them do to you, for this sums up the Law and the Prophets" (Matthew 7:12 NIV).

So, there is a rule, but it is not a rule that saves us or makes us spiritual. It is a rule to always love and act in love. John the Apostle taught us that only those who are in Christ have the capacity to love the way God loves.

> Dear friends, let us love one another, for love comes from God. Everyone who loves has been born of God and knows God. Whoever does not love does not know God, because God is love. This is how God showed his love among us: He sent his one and only Son into the world that we might live through him. This is love: not that we loved God, but that he loved us and sent his Son as an atoning sacrifice for our sins. Dear friends, since God so loved us, we also ought to love one another. No one has ever seen God; but if we love one another, God lives in us and his love is made complete in us. (1 John 4:7–12 NIV)

Many misquote this passage when they declare, "God is a god of love." While that is true, our God is so much more. He is love. He lives in us. His delight is to live his love through us, his children. Clearly, we are responsible to live his love in all we say and do; it is also obvious that we cannot accomplish this love apart from him.

I hope we can see a difference between this rule and those that "lay down the law" of oppression on us. Love means we are free to live unselfish, caring, giving lives that benefit others. As long as we are living love, nothing is off limits to us. However, to respond without love opens the door to our flesh, our sin nature.

Here is the problem as I see it. I am totally incapable of making myself a loving individual. Keeping the rules will not make me loving. I have tried and failed. My strength is not enough. Even at my very best, I am reminded of Isaiah's words: "All of us have become like one who is unclean, and all our righteous acts are like filthy rags; we all shrivel up like a leaf, and like the wind our sins sweep us away" (64:6 NIV).

There must be something more, something better. There is. I hope it will excite you as much as it does me.

CHAPTER 29

THE BIG PICTURE

Sometimes it is hard to see the forest for the trees. Focusing on the smaller things, we fail to see the big picture. Rules are that way. Focusing on the individual instructions can keep our attention off the aim of what the rules are to accomplish, that is, loving one another.

Here is our whole goal as children of God as told by our Savior: "Jesus replied: 'Love the Lord your God with all your heart and with all your soul and with all your mind.' This is the first and greatest commandment. And the second is like it: 'Love your neighbor as yourself.' All the Law and the Prophets hang on these two commandments" (Matt. 22:37–40 NIV).

When Jesus was asked, "Who is my neighbor?" He answered with the story of the Good Samaritan (Luke 10:29–37).

> In reply Jesus said: "A man was going down from Jerusalem to Jericho, when he was attacked by robbers. They stripped him of his clothes, beat him and went away, leaving him half dead. A priest happened to be going down the same road, and when he saw the man, he passed by on the other side. So too, a Levite, when he came to the place and saw him, passed by on the other side. But a Samaritan, as he traveled,

> came where the man was; and when he saw him, he took pity on him. He went to him and bandaged his wounds, pouring on oil and wine. Then he put the man on his own donkey, brought him to an inn and took care of him. The next day he took out two denarii and gave them to the innkeeper. 'Look after him,' he said, 'and when I return, I will reimburse you for any extra expense you may have.' 'Which of these three do you think was a neighbor to the man who fell into the hands of robbers?' The expert in the law replied, 'The one who had mercy on him.' Jesus told him, 'Go and do likewise.'" (Luke 10:30–37 NIV)

The conclusion we draw from the story is our neighbor can be not just those we know, but people in need whom we have never met before. To me, my neighbor includes my fellow Christian brothers and sisters: "A new command I give you: Love one another. As I have loved you, so you must love one another. By this everyone will know that you are my disciples, if you love one another" (John 13:34–35 NIV).

My neighbors also include my enemies. Again, here are the words of Jesus: "You have heard that it was said, 'Love your neighbor and hate your enemy.' But I tell you, love your enemies and pray for those who persecute you, that you may be children of your Father in heaven. He causes his sun to rise on the evil and the good, and sends rain on the righteous and the unrighteous. If you love those who love you, what reward will you get? Are not even the tax collectors doing that?" (Matthew 5:43–46 NIV).

What does it mean to love my neighbor as myself? Far too many of us don't love ourselves, but there are a few things I know about self-love. I loved myself to such a great degree that I wanted and received God's gift of eternal life. This has become my desire for other people and has stimulated me to try to share Christ with those who do not know him.

I love myself so much I want God's peace to rule in my heart. I need the assurance of my home in heaven. I find encouragement for living in the truth of God's word. This should define my love for people with spiritual needs.

I need prayer, lots of prayer support, to walk closely with Christ. Should I love others any less?

I love myself so much that I want three square meals and a warm place to sleep. This should define my attitude toward the poor, homeless, and needy. I want to be healthy and have my medical needs met.

I cannot do everything for everyone. Sometimes, the needs are so many and my ability so small. How do I demonstrate love knowing my neighbor has a need only my God can meet? Can I offer a "breath prayer" (a prayer that only takes a breath) on their behalf?

I do not want to be judged by others, so why would I allow myself to be judgmental? Well, I guess I'm admitting one of my weaknesses. Sometimes I get hit right between the eyes when I realize my duty is to love, not to judge.

I hope we all get the idea that the "rule we can live with" is a lifestyle. It is a manner of life available to us only through our walk with our God. It is a relationship with our God who is love.

CHAPTER 30

OUR MARCHING ORDERS!

Is the Christian life hard? How has it been going lately? As I evaluate my life, I think it is about as hard as I make it. Really, though I know there is a war going on between my flesh and the Spirit, I really don't think God intended it to be as hard as I make it.

Though the origin of the story of two dogs living inside us in dispute, it does, nevertheless, well illustrate the conflict we feel within us. As the story is told, an adult Native American told his son, "'Inside of man there are two dogs. One is mean and evil and the other is good. The evil dog fights the good dog all the time.' When asked which dog wins, he thought for a moment, then replied, 'The dog I feed the most.'"

Paul puts it in different words. Let's see if we can identify with what he says. "So I say, walk by the Spirit, and you will not gratify the desires of the flesh. For the flesh desires what is contrary to the Spirit, and the Spirit what is contrary to the flesh. They are in conflict with each other, so that you are not to do whatever you want. But if you are led by the Spirit, you are not under the law" (Galatians 5:16–19 NIV). I guess the question now is, "Who are we going to feed?" Feed the flesh, gratify its desires. Feed the Spirit, experience our own Declaration of Independence! Still, we know it is not that easy, not that cut and dried.

Let's face it, sin is fun. It is much more appealing because our old nature craves it. We read our Bibles, pray as much as we can, attend every church service we can; and we still struggle. The battle rages on. What are we to do?

For me, and others I know, I came to the point where I confessed, "God, I cannot change my heart. If my heart is ever going to change, you will have to do it." And he did. How?

God has incorporated into our being the ability to choose. We call it free will. Yet when we choose his will, he incorporates his sovereign will, that is, God does what only God can do. He changes us. Our choice to "walk by the Spirit" results in God freeing us from the rules. Who needs rules when it is not in our nature to break them? Our old nature is suppressed by the Spirit of God as we conduct our lives according to his will.

The idea of "walking" with the Spirit means to behave ourselves the way the Spirit directs us. It is not a one-time deal. In the original language, this walk is not a stroll down the lane, but a continual walk step-by-step day in, day out continual journey. It is not even one day at a time, it is one step at a time.

> But if you are led by the Spirit the acts of the flesh are obvious: sexual immorality, impurity and debauchery; idolatry and witchcraft; hatred, discord, jealousy, fits of rage, selfish ambition, dissensions, factions and envy; drunkenness, orgies, and the like. I warn you, as I did before, that those who live like this will not inherit the kingdom of God. (Galatians 5:18–22 NIV)

Wow! Those of us who are walking in the Spirit are led by the Spirit. He never leads us to do the "acts of the flesh." Those acts are obvious to us. He names them. They sound like rules, but if we are walking in the Spirit, we are free from the rules.

We immediately recognize the promptings of our sin nature. God changes our hearts! These works of the flesh lose their appeal the closer we walk with the Spirit.

What will our lives look like when we are walking in the Spirit? "But the fruit of the Spirit is love, joy, peace, forbearance, kindness, goodness, faithfulness, gentleness and self-control. Against such things there is no law" (Galatians 5:22–24 NIV).

I never could generate or manufacture these traits. I think every preacher I've heard has preached on this passage, myself included. I haven't been able to make myself love. I can't force joy or peace into my life. The harder I try, the harder my life becomes.

When God began to change my heart, one of the first things I noticed was my love for others. I became more at peace in my life and found joy in just living. I've always wanted to write, but when I'd think about it, I realized I did not have the self-control to stick with it. Things have changed!

"Those who belong to Christ Jesus have crucified the flesh with its passions and desires. Since we live by the Spirit, let us keep in step with the Spirit" (Galatians 5:24– 25 NIV). Here is a fact we are to believe. The power of faith is ours through our saving relationship with Christ.

Believe the truth: We have crucified, killed, put to death our old nature. "I have been crucified with Christ and I no longer live, but Christ lives in me. The life I now live in the body, I live by faith in the Son of God, who loved me and gave himself for me" (Galatians 2:20–21 NIV).

Paul repeats, "Since we live by the Spirit," since this is our manner of living, "keep in step with the Spirit." "Keep in step" is a military term meaning to walk or march in line. You know, "Left, left, left right left!" Keeping in step with the Spirit is "our marching orders," our cadence.

As strange as it sounds, we win by surrendering. I would never discourage anyone from doing the Christian basics: read and study the Bible, pray, go to church, have Christian friends, etc. We will benefit and grow as we do these, but they are the basics.

But I did this—and more than you can imagine—to conquer my flesh, but failed. I failed to the point of utter desolation. Panic and anxiety attacks plagued me. Depression was a constant companion. But from the depths of despair, I surrendered to him and learned how to praise him in everything.

CHAPTER 31

AN ATTITUDE ADJUSTMENT

In our study, "Our Spiritual Declaration of Independence," we have learned we have been set free by God's grace to the laws or rules we build our lives around. We can enslave ourselves to them, or we can live by the Spirit. That life constitutes "our marching orders."

God gives us the control in our lives to choose to walk in step with the Spirit. When we do, he makes changes in us he calls the fruit of the Spirit. As I try to explain this "divine/human cooperative," the only way I know to do it is to dip deeply into my personal story.

Some people call this an attitude adjustment. I admit I lived selfishly, self-centered, and self-absorbed. Consequently, my focus was me stopping my rule-breaking tendencies, finding strength for my weaknesses, and help in my struggles. As I've shared earlier, I was losing.

There came a time when I gave up trying. You might say I gave up on God. I couldn't read my Bible or pray. I did not go to church. I started doing things I knew were bad for me and things I had never done before. I threw off restraint. I was depressed, and life was getting darker every day.

If you have ever thought about giving up on God, let me tell you, it doesn't work! If you are a child of God, you may give up on him, but he never gives up on you. You think it is bad now? Just wait, it can get a lot worse. Trust me. I know by experience.

I describe my ensuing depression as a "black hole." In scientific theory, a stellar black hole is a sun that reached the end of its life and collapses in on itself. It becomes so dense that its gravity grows so strong it will not allow anything to escape, not even light.

That is pretty well the best description I can find to help you relate to the darkness of my depression. I was on mood stabilizers, antidepressants, anti-anxiety prescriptions, and other medications to help me manage the bipolar disorder with which I wrestle. To be fair, I'm still on them, because God has not taken the disorder away. The medications only give me the ability to manage the disorder. The rest is up to me by changing the way I think

My only thought I had was the pain I felt. Of course, the more I thought about it, the more I hurt. You see, it is not easier to give up. As I ran from God, I took my greatest adversary with me. His name is Charlie.

It was during this time that God put in my hands a little book written by a United Methodist Church minister about the subject of giving thanks. What I learned from the Scriptures after repeated readings of that short book gave me the attitude adjustment that changed my life.

Wise believers know God's will for his children is that we be filled with the Holy Spirit. Paul's description of the believer's life in Christ in Ephesians is quite similar to those in Galatians 5. He tells us to walk in love (verse 2), not in the flesh (verse 3–7), to walk as children of light (verse 8), not darkness (verse 9–12).

> Be very careful, then, how you live—not as unwise but as wise… do not be foolish, but understand what the Lord's will is. Do not get drunk on wine, which leads to debauchery. Instead, be filled with the Spirit, speaking to one another with

psalms, hymns, and songs from the Spirit. Sing and make music from your heart to the Lord, always giving thanks to God the Father for everything, in the name of our Lord Jesus Christ. (Ephesians 5:15, 17–20 NIV).

The truths of giving praise and thanksgiving are closely related to our walk with the Holy Spirit that frees us from the rules. As a matter of fact, and please don't miss this, in my case they provided the doorway for the "filling of the Spirit." Being filled with the Spirit and walking in the Spirit is the same truth.

When we are drunk on alcohol, we are controlled by it. Alcohol lowers inhibitions and allows a drunk person to do what he really wanted to do all along but did not have the courage to do. Instead, be controlled by the Holy Spirit.

This is given to us in the form of a command. In other words, we have a choice to be filled or not be filled. What can I do to get the Spirit to fill and control me? Do you feel your frustration level going up?

The answer is right here in this passage. There are two elements: singing and giving thanks. He describes the singing with four different words. The first is *psalms*. The book of Psalms was the Jewish songbook for worship. Some were for times of joy, others for sorrow, or any other expression of emotion we may experience.

The second is *hymns*. These are songs of praise to God. In Acts 16:25, Paul and Silas were singing these songs of praise the night the earthquake shook their stocks loose and opened the prison doors.

"Spiritual songs" (KJV) comprise the third group. New songs have always been written through the centuries to reflect the time, culture, and experience of believers as we relate to scriptural truth. I think these types of songs, which began appearing in Paul's writings, fall into this group of music.

Lastly, we are to "sing and make melody in our hearts to the Lord." This is praise singing accompanied by instruments, particularly stringed instruments.

To boil it all down to one idea, wise believers filled with Spirit *praise God*! We praise him in song to the benefit of our fellow believers. This goes along so closely to Hebrews 10:25, "Not giving up meeting together, as some are in the habit of doing, but encouraging one another—and all the more as you see the Day approaching." It sounds like the encouragement is as much us encouraging others as it is them encouraging us.

The second thing we are told to do is to "always giving thanks to God the Father for everything in the name of our Lord Jesus Christ." Did you catch that little word: *for*? I'm sorry. *For* means "for." Some have told me that they don't have that kind of faith. Too much has happened that they are not thankful for. All I can say is the choice to be thankful is up to everyone. The question I need to ask myself is, "Am I filled with the Holy Spirit?"

The word for giving thanks is one we might be slightly familiar with. It is a matter of giving the gift of grace, thanks, to God. It is the acknowledgement on our part that no matter how dark or bad our circumstances may be, it is designed by our God for our good.

I have confessed before that I have bipolar disorder (I am not bipolar—there is a difference). Hating the disorder made me its victim. With all its varied manifestations, it was difficult for me to live with the compulsions and the choices I had made.

I hated my circumstances, the place I lived, the job I had, and the food I ate. I was miserable, and the attempts I made to please myself left me feeling empty and alone.

Though I had been a pastor and knew what God said about praise and thanksgiving, it was because of that little book, I decided to put it into practice. I began praising God, worshipping him, and thanking him for everything. I was no longer a victim of my disorder or circumstances. I became a victor over them! Instead of moaning about how unfair it was to be saddled with bipolar disorder, I began to give thanks to my God for it. Rather than curse my weaknesses, I gave him praise because as Paul told the Corinthians, "For when I am weak, then I am strong" (2 Corinthians 12:10 NIV).

The victory wasn't instantaneous, but I grew as I gave thanks to my God. Eventually, my attitude changed. I have become happier, more peaceful, more loving to others and less self-preoccupied. Whereas before I couldn't say no to my flesh, self-control has grown in its place.

In short, God is growing the fruit of the Spirit in me, and I didn't even try to make it happen. What changed was my attitude. When the darkness of depression or temptations enters my mind, the Holy Spirit is quick to remind me to praise him and to offer thanks for what has come my way.

We are so blessed in America with a great abundance of Christian radio stations. We have three we can pick up where I live. One is K-LOVE, a nationwide radio network. I took their challenge a while back to listen to nothing but Christian music for thirty days. I've never looked back. When I travel, I plug in Pandora to my car radio and choose a praise channel. I am continually blessed.

I haven't mentioned digging into God's word or prayer as solutions for the filling of the Spirit. These two activities began to grow again in my life after learning to praise him. We might all do well to start with praise.

PART 6

LIVING THE LIFE OF LOVE

CHAPTER 32

A MORE EXCELLENT WAY

There are two truths that have become a never-ending source of amazement to me. It hasn't always been this way, but God has never failed to teach me in his school of understanding. The first truth is his amazing, unconditional love for us. The other is His plans for us to love others using His love as our model.

He told us very clearly who we are to love: him first, neighbors, ourselves, enemies, and one another. That pretty well covers everyone. We work hard to come up with exceptions, especially when loving some people are particularly difficult. But it doesn't matter who it is, God loves even the ones we find unlovable.

Any human definition of love falls short of giving us a clear understanding. We are blessed because God in his infinite wisdom has defined it for us in the perfect way. He wrote 1 Corinthians 13:1–13.

> If I speak in the tongues of men or of angels, but do not have love, I am only a resounding gong or a clanging cymbal. If I have the gift of prophecy and can fathom all mysteries and all knowledge, and if I have a faith that can move mountains, but do not have love, I am nothing. If I give all I possess to the poor and give

> over my body to hardship that I may boast, but do not have love, I gain nothing.
>
> Love is patient, love is kind. It does not envy, it does not boast, it is not proud. It does not dishonor others, it is not self-seeking, it is not easily angered, it keeps no record of wrongs. Love does not delight in evil but rejoices with the truth. It always protects, always trusts, always hopes, always perseveres.
>
> Love never fails. But where there are prophecies, they will cease; where there are tongues, they will be stilled; where there is knowledge, it will pass away. For we know in part and we prophesy in part, but when completeness comes, what is in part disappears. When I was a child, I talked like a child, I thought like a child, I reasoned like a child. When I became a man, I put the ways of childhood behind me. For now we see only a reflection as in a mirror; then we shall see face to face. Now I know in part; then I shall know fully, even as I am fully known.
>
> And now these three remain: faith, hope and love. But the greatest of these is love. (NIV)

Now, if any of us just glossed over that passage of scripture, let's go back and really read it for understanding and comprehension. These thirteen verses are probably second only to Psalm 23 in the all-time most memorized chapters in the Bible.

I think most of us will concede that 1 Corinthians 13 is an ideal for us to follow. My heart gets a little heavy (maybe a lot heavier!) when I think of the people who have gotten under my skin and my response was anything but loving. There were too many people I simply did not love.

Before we break this chapter down over the next few chapters, I must admit this description of *love* is a bit daunting. It seems so far out there as to not be even humanly possible. That is a correct conclusion! It is not.

John the Apostle tells us we only have this capacity through a saving relationship with our Lord Jesus Christ. We have visited this passage in this book before, but a reminder might be good for us.

> Dear friends, let us love one another, for love comes from God. Everyone who loves has been born of God and knows God. Whoever does not love does not know God, because God is love. This is how God showed his love: not that we loved God, but that he loved us and sent his Son as an atoning sacrifice for our sins. Dear friends, since God so loved us, we also ought to love one another. No one has ever seen God; but if we love one another, God lives in us and his love is made complete in us…God is love. Whoever lives in love lives in God, and God in them…We love because he first loved us. (1 John 4:7–12, 16, 19; NIV)

As we studied in the topic of "Our Spiritual Declaration of Independence," we learned love is a decision we can make. It is possible only as we walk in the Spirit. John teaches us that we cannot be any more like our Lord than when we love one another.

In a particularly difficult period in my life, I met with a pastor, hoping to receive some sort of encouragement. I was struggling with my, as of yet, unidentified mental illness; and my behavior was bizarre, to say the least. My hurting family had sent a discouraging message: If I really wanted to change, I would. Their conclusion was, I must not really want to change.

Feeling the frustration of having tried and failed countless times, I sighed. "If only I could be loved unconditionally, just as I am." The pastor looked at me quizzically, then said, "Charlie, isn't all love conditional?" Well, in my experience that seemed true.

Thankfully, that is not the way God loves us. Nor is it the way we must love. Like Paul says, "And yet I will show you the most excellent way" (1 Corinthians 12:31 NIV).

CHAPTER 33

FOR ALL THE RIGHT REASONS

The English language is so limited. We use the word *love* to describe our preferences, our passions, friends, family, and our lifelong partner. It is an excellent example of why our language is so difficult to understand. A person may say, "I love chocolate," while another admits, "I love my dog." My barber put it rather crudely when he said, "Young people today think they are in love when they are really just in heat!" He could have said that about adults as well.

It could be confusing if we approached the Bible with such a varied understanding of the word *love*. Fortunately, God deliberately eliminated that problem for us. As the Spirit of God moved in Paul the Apostle to write his love language to us in 1 Corinthians 13, he could have chosen from a variety of Greek words we would translate as *love*.

The word choice God used is limited in its expression of emotional or passionate emphasis. God's love may express itself in these manners depending on our relationship with one another. For example, husbands are commanded to love their wives, and emotion and passion will be a part of that love.

When we love one another as we are commanded, we will form emotional attachments. However, the choice to love our enemies may well precede any emotional experience. As such, the decision to love must override any issue we have with this person. We need a peg to hang our definition on. What, then, is the meaning of the love found in 1 Corinthians 13?

Though the Greeks had four different words we would use the English word *love* to translate, only two are used in the New Testament. The first is *phileo*, which describes the relationship between friends. To express God's highest form of love, he uses the word *agape*. The central meaning of *agape* is "give." You see, relationships between friends can change. Giving is a forever commitment.

"For God so loved the world that he gave his one and only Son, that whoever believes in him shall not perish but have eternal life" (John 3:16 NIV). "But God demonstrates his own love for us in this: While we were still sinners, Christ died for us" (Romans 5:8 NIV). "Greater love has no one than this: to lay down one's life for one's friends" (John 15:13 NIV).

God's love for us required that he gave of himself to purchase our salvation. While eternal life cost us nothing, God gave his Son to die in our place. Why did he do such a thing? The cross demonstrated his magnificent love for us. This giving of ourselves to others is possible; he implanted that capacity in us (1 John 4:13–21).

Paul lets us know that we can do about anything with the wrong motives or attitudes. No matter how well we perform, we gain nothing without love. In fact, he says we are nothing. I can be the best at what I am called to do but fall short of gaining any lasting value if I operate without love. Let's reread what Paul wrote about the importance of love.

> If I speak in the tongues of men or of angels, but do not have love, I am only a resounding gong or a

> clanging cymbal. If I have the gift of prophecy and can fathom all mysteries and all knowledge, and if I have a faith that can move mountains, but do not have love, I am nothing. If I give all I possess to the poor and give over my body to hardship that I may boast, but do not have love, I gain nothing. (1 Corinthians 13:1–3 NIV)

Paul introduced the subject of spiritual gifts in 1 Corinthians 12. From the gifts he named, he used a few specific illustrations of spiritual gifts so we might understand the importance of love. The Corinthians believers thought speaking in tongues was the most important, but Paul says, "No matter how impressive you are, without love you are just a noise maker." Whoa! That is sobering! The gift of prophesy, in this context, was the ability to receive and deliver a message directly from God. This was exceptionally important since they did not have a completed New Testament to study. Understanding all mysteries and all presented revelation would be awesome!

When I think of the hours, days, weeks, months, and years of study a Bible teacher spends to gain the best understanding possible, it would be great to shortcut that process. I spent most of my ministry thinking I had the answers, only to now realize I don't even know what the questions were!

As we have studied elsewhere, faith is essential to our Christian walk. Believing God above all else is our commissioning in life if it is exercised with love. People could stand in awe as we trust God to move mountains in our lives, but we are nothing without love. For me, I would be no more than a flash in the pan.

Yet with all that effort invested in the presentation of the truth, exercising all the faith possible, this can all be done without love. God's has promised, "My word that goes out from my mouth: It will not return to me empty, but will accomplish what I desire and achieve the purpose for which I sent it" (Isaiah 55:11 NIV). His word will always hit the mark he intended when he leads his messenger to speak. After all, he did speak through Balaam's donkey!

While attempting to minister God's word without love, I know I have walked away thinking either, *Wow! That was good!* or *I'm wasted! I've failed.* If the motive isn't love, the most important ingredient is missing from the message.

Maybe I should mention that the ministry of the Word is a two-way street. We can listen without love and go away saying, "I didn't get anything out of their preaching." I used to be a difficult pew sitter to speak to. While I tried not to be critical of other preachers, I really was in my heart. Pride is a terrible fault.

As God changed my heart and I learned to listen for his voice through his speaker, I noticed something amazing: love. This is especially true with our current pastor. He is twenty years my junior and in his first pastorate while completing his seminary degree. His love for our Savior is so evident and his love for all of us is almost tangible. God is using him greatly! We love him dearly!

Paul goes as far as to say that our most sacrificial acts can be performed without love. We can sell all our possessions, thereby becoming poor and homeless ourselves, to give the proceeds to other poor people—all the while doing it with the wrong motives and attitudes. We may even voluntarily subject ourselves to abuse for Christ's name's sake—all for the wrong reasons.

Paul did all those things and confessed that if love were missing, he said, "I gain nothing." He did not say, "I accomplish nothing." No, he says, "It has no value for me."

I identify with that. For years, I struggled to wisely and intelligently present the word of God to his people. I pressed for God's people to make commitments to him. I cannot say I failed because to do so would mean that God's word failed. Yet I know I failed to operate my spiritual gifts with love. After so many years having served without love, with the wrong motives and attitudes, I believe God gave me a fresh start not too many years ago. You know, one of those blessed "do overs."

"For God's gifts and his call are irrevocable" (Rom. 11:29 NIV). God never says, "Charlie, I'm sorry I saved you. I'm sorry I called you to preach My word." The rewards of fulfillment now, and eternal dividends later, come only by loving God first and then loving people.

This love is an investment into other people's lives. It is serving for all the right reasons. It is a bonding of souls where we give ourselves for the good of others. his love forms an emotion attachment and creates a passion to help, to be involved in one another's lives. It is risky, dangerous, and potentially painful. It is a growing process that will motivate energies we did not know we had.

Love is just that: An investment into the lives of other people. Why would I want to do that? Remember, please, love is what happens when we yield ourselves to the control of the Holy Spirit. God's fruit manifests itself as we walk with him.

It goes without saying that this outgrowth of God's design is only for those who desire to walk with him. Whew, let me tell you! It sure beats the alternative of the emptiness of a heart not fully devoted to the Savior.

CHAPTER 34

A PANORAMIC PICTURE OF LOVE

The often-asked question through generations has been, "How can I know if I am really in love?" For a young guy, I would think I was in love when the object of my affection would appear, my throat would become dry, I stumbled over my words, I lost my appetite, and I would duck away from shyness.

I know now that all I was experiencing was infatuation. Love is so much more. One day the butterflies fly away. The stumbling words begin to flow, and words come out we really wish had not. Sometimes we stay away not out of shyness but maybe out of fatigue. All the emotion flees, but love, agape love, remains.

We have learned that love is a commitment of the gift of ourselves to others. Real love comes out of our relationship with Christ. To be fair, as a human being made in the image of God, we may all love because "He first loved us." But "love comes from God. Everyone who loves has been born of God and knows God" (1 John 4:7 NIV).

We have grown in our relationship with our Lord. We are led by the Holy Spirit, filled with the Spirit. The fruit of the Spirit has blossomed and ripened out of our walking in step with him. God gives us a panoramic picture of what Spirit love looks like.

> Love is patient, love is kind. It does not envy, it does not boast, it is not proud. It does not dishonor others, it is not self-seeking, it is not easily angered, it keeps no record of wrongs. Love does not delight in evil but rejoices with the truth. It always protects, always trusts, always hopes, always perseveres. Love never fails. (1 Corinthians 13:4–8 NIV)

God uses Paul to detail his love in both positive and negative ways. The scope of love is so beautifully and majestically described as to be breathtaking in its presentation. It's like I tell my Sunday school class, "I'm so excited that I have goose bumps on my goose bumps!"

This passage does not merely tell us what love does, but it describes the character of love. They are the components of love. When we look at an object, let's say a car, we do not lift the hood, point to the engine, and say, "That is a car." Rather, we look at the fully assembled vehicle and say, "Now, there is a car!"

Similarly, we see these characteristics of love in action and declare, "Now, that is love!" We know from Scripture what love is and what it is not. We can accurately understand the love God has given for us to live. So, if we are painting a picture of love, what will it look like?

Paul leads with two positive affirmations of this fantastic love that is ours to possess. "Love is patient, love is kind." When this was written, the literal meaning of the word *patient* is "to be long tempered." The best definition I have ever read comes from an early childhood Bible curriculum we used with our children: "*Patience* is 'the ability to wait with a quiet spirit.'"

Paul shares the opposite of this attribute in this passage as well. Love "is not easily angered." If you are like me, I am very prone to fly off the handle when things don't go my way. Very soon afterward I will be extremely sorry and apologetic. As the fruit of the Spirit continues to flourish in me (you know, "love, joy, peace, patience" [Gal. 5:22, NASB]), my ability to wait with a quiet spirit continues to grow.

Secondly, Paul says that "love is kind." Interestingly enough, kindness is also part of the fruit of the Spirit, just like patience. Kindness is seen when we do good for those we love (everyone we can, our "neighbor"). The root word is sometimes translated *goodness* or, as the King James Version says, *gentleness*.

After listing several traits absent from love, which we will examine in our next discussion, Paul continues the positive characteristics of love. Love "rejoices with the truth. It always protects, always trusts, always hopes, always perseveres. Love never fails" (1 Corinthians 13:6–8 NIV).

"Rejoices with the truth" is reminiscent of Ephesians 4:15, "speaking the truth in love." As I have meditated on this idea, I came to realize just how broad the implications are to rejoice in the truth. We hide a part of ourselves from others because we think, "*If you really knew me, you wouldn't like me, let alone love me.*" Love sets aside all judgment concerning who we are or who we perceive ourselves and others to be. Rather, we rejoice in the trust we share to just accept each other as we are.

Truth may not be what we want to hear, but truth is far preferable over any lie to the contrary. God's word is truth, and at times, it exposes things we don't want to know. Sometimes we feel convicted to share truth with others who do not want to know it, but in all cases, love compels us on.

Love also "always protects." Literally this means "to protect by covering." We can easily understand this protection extends to our children, spouse, loved ones, and friends. For these, we would sacrifice ourselves out of love. But there is a figurative sense of "love protecting by covering."

"Above all, love each other deeply, because love covers over a multitude of sins" (1 Peter 4:8–9 NIV). What is our attitude when we hear of someone else's sin? Or when we see it? "Remember this: Whoever turns a sinner from the error of their way will save them from death and cover over a multitude of sins" (James 5:20 NIV).

Love protects by covering. In love, we invest ourselves in reclaiming an erring soul. No broadcasts of the wrong doings of others can be considered an act of love. Love does not say, "I'm sharing this with you because I know you'll pray, but don't tell anyone else." Love protects others from judgment.

"Love always trusts" or "believes." I don't think that means love is gullible. Rather, love believes in others. Some have forfeited the right to be believed because of their lies, but love never gives up on the liar. Love believes the other person can change by the grace of God. It is that unshakable faith that God loves others so much he will do what no one else can. Love declares, "I believe in you! I believe you can succeed!"

"Love always hopes." Hope is the "expectation of good." Instead of being pessimistic, looking for failure in others, love looks for the good in people. Isn't this a transformation from what we have conditioned ourselves to believe?

"Love always perseveres." It doesn't give up. The word means to "remain under the load." It is the strength of character that keeps going in the face of hardship. Love becomes the great encourager in our lives as we encounter others who try our patience.

Finally, "love never fails." It never bows down and collapses beneath the load. Do circumstance or people ever break my spirit? It is love that will pick me up and usher me on my way. Taking all the characteristics of love into consideration, love is you and I living the life of Christ into lives of those around us.

My friends, I cannot make this kind of love grow into my life. I don't have the strength. It is against my human nature. But I don't have to make it happen. The only thing I can control is my walk with the Holy Spirit. When I am filled with the Spirit, God produces the fruit of the Spirit.

It is a good life. God did it all. Love beats being a hater any day of the week.

CHAPTER 35

LIVING LOVE DAILY

Jesus taught us to treat others the way we want others to treat us. We call it the golden rule. While studying 1 Corinthians 13, I realized the love we see in this passage is not just the way I am supposed to love others, but it is the way I want to be loved. Just like God's love for me, it is a perfect unconditional love.

Even at my very worst condition, God never gave up on me. He has always believed in me. He has put people in my life during those ugly times whose love for me has never failed.

During my "black hole" periods, on more than one occasion, my thinking was so dark, I opted to attempt to end my life. I took massive overdoses of muscle-relaxing drugs or psychiatric medications with the expectation that I would not wake up. I figured people who loved me were better off without me.

I'm so thankful those attempts failed, and they are now part of my history. Each time, I woke up in the hospital. Each time meant a prolonged stay in the psych ward. Each time, my oldest son visited me and said, "I don't know why this happened, but you are my dad, and I decided that I love you and I forgive you." This is unconditional love.

Just as there are elements present in this *agape* love, which prompts us to give of ourselves and to accept people just as they are, there is also at least one thing that is conspicuous by its absence. We are given a list of unlovely features that mar relationships. They can be summarized in one thought. Love is characterized by the total lack of self-interest. This is living love daily. It's where the rubber meets the road and we are faced with real-life situations.

> It does not envy, it does not boast, it is not proud. It does not dishonor others, it is not self-seeking, it is not easily angered, it keeps no record of wrongs. Love does not delight in evil. (1 Corinthians 13:4–6 NIV)

Envy or jealousy is best defined as "the feelings of displeasure over the success of others or what someone else has." As a minister of the Gospel of Jesus Christ, I had an issue with envy. If another preacher had success, I would let the feelings of, "why couldn't that be me?" eat at my soul. I had been a pastor more than ten years before God settled this issue in my heart.

The Holy Spirit led me to speak at a Bible conference to preachers on the topic "God Called Us to Cooperate, Not Compete." An evangelist met me afterward, laid his hand on my shoulder, and wept, "I am so competitive." I guess I wasn't alone. Love removes self from the equation.

Love "does not brag, it is not proud…it is not self-seeking." It is so easy to buy into our societies' practice of believing we really are "number one." "Hey, look at me! See what I did!" We watch others move up the ladder, maybe even taking credit for our work, and we feel violated. Why? Are we thinking, "*It should have been ME!*"

That illustration is not even fair! Too many of us have experienced that. I can only speak for myself. At those times, I really have considered myself better, more deserving, or more important. It leads to envy. And it is not love.

Our Bibles have a lot to say about the subject of bragging, self-seeking, and pride. We can hardly read the book of Proverbs without being confronted by these topics. Love places others above ourselves. "Do nothing out of selfish ambition or vain conceit. Rather, in humility value others above yourselves, not looking to your own interests but each of you to the interests of the others" (Philippians 2:3–5 NIV).

Paul tells us that there is a proper way to think about ourselves. "For by the grace given me I say to every one of you: Do not think of yourself more highly than you ought, but rather think of yourself with sober judgment, in accordance with the faith God has distributed to each of you" (Romans 12:3 NIV). There is a balance. We are uniquely placed in the Body of Christ to serve others to the best of our ability. It is to cop out to believe we have little to offer.

I can be a very sarcastic person with a biting tongue. Frankly, I find it can be a socially acceptable form of bullying that brings laughter at the expense of others. But love "does not dishonor others." You know, when I remember how much I've been hurt by the biting humor of others, I am quite ashamed that I allow myself to fall into that trap.

Love "keeps no record of wrong." We are good at record keeping. Get in an argument, and as things get heated. We digress into "trading verbal punches." Instead of discussion, we can so easily recite all those wrongs the other person has perpetrated. Here we are, being plummeted by offences we thought were already forgiven!

As a child, I was raised by the switch my mom used and by the belt my dad wore. Mind you, I was not the perfect child. Once, it had been a while since I had received a trip to the garage (we didn't have a woodshed). With each slap of my dad's belt, he called out another infraction, "This one is for breaking your sister's doll. This one is for taking the spring out of my shotgun. This one is for—" I had accumulated quite a record! I know my dad loved me, but it was not love that prompted using a score card!

Finally, love "does not delight in evil." I'll admit, I have real issues here because while I may hang my head and ache in my heart for the evil one human being perpetrates on another, much of my entertainment revolves around TV shows that deal with similar subjects. I am learning to love more every day. I soothe my mind by saying, "It's just fiction. It's not real." But is it love?

Maybe it is a good idea to mention that love doesn't mean letting people walk all over us or never taking a stand when we are wronged. So, that we may balance this out, remember love does not rejoice in wrongdoing, but it does rejoice in the truth. Love doesn't give up on the person doing wrong to us. Sometime the most loving thing we can do for both the other person and ourselves is to say, "Why are you saying this? Have I harmed you in some way?" or "I don't think I deserve this treatment."

I want to walk with the Lord Jesus. I want to live as he wants me to. I want his Spirit living in me to control me and produce his fruit. Love is not only the first characteristic of that fruit of the Spirit that is mentioned in Galatians 5:21–22, I believe love is revealed through the eight other descriptions of that fruit.

So, we walk in the Spirit, and I'll admit with you that I'm not there yet. Love is being matured, but I've got a way to go. What does God tell us about that?

CHAPTER 36

LOVE LASTS

A little bit of knowledge can be a dangerous thing in the hands of the immature. Omar Khayyam, the thirteenth- century Persian philosopher, is credited with saying:

> He who knows not, and knows not that he knows not, is a fool. Shun him.
>
> He who knows not, and knows that he knows not, is a child. Teach him.
>
> He who knows, and knows not that he knows, is asleep. Wake him.
>
> He who knows, and knows that he knows, is a leader. Follow him.

I chuckle when I think about my early years in ministry. I was opinionated, hard-headed, obstinate, and convinced that I was doing the will of God through all my mistakes! This even applied to my mechanical aptitude. There was no automotive problem I would not tackle only to end up messing up things royally. I did some engine work for a parishioner once. He said, "Pastor, you are heck of a good preacher but one lousy mechanic!" Oops!

Part of maturity is recognizing we have not yet arrived. Maybe we "know that we know not." Perhaps we "know that we know" but still need to grow. This is where I find myself as we consider 1 Corinthians 13. Once, this love seemed too ideal, too out of reach, too unlike me. Since I pushed it aside. I didn't measure up; I threw away the measuring stick. How convenient!

The Holy Spirit is so awesome! When we learned about "our Spiritual Declaration of Independence," God revealed our lives are to be governed by his love energized in us and not by rules. Living controlled by the Spirit produces the fruit of the Spirit in us, which begins with love.

Desiring to walk with my Savior has been an adventure, but when I walked in my flesh, I can safely say I was selfish, self-centered, and insecure. I did not love myself and was too wrapped up in trying to soothe my bruised soul to love others the way I was designed by God to do.

Since God, by his amazing grace, turned my heart around, the growth in living his love through me has become a fascinating journey. It has been and will continue to be a maturing experience. Please follow this idea with me from the "Love" chapter.

> But where there are prophecies, they will cease; where there are tongues, they will be stilled; where there is knowledge, it will pass away. For we know in part and we prophesy in part, but when completeness comes, what is in part disappears. When I was a child, I talked like a child, I thought like a child, I reasoned like a child. When I became a man, I put the ways of childhood behind me. For now, we see only a reflection as in a mirror; then we shall see face to face. Now I know in part; then I shall know fully, even as I am fully

> known. And now these three remain: faith, hope and love. But the greatest of these is love. (1 Corinthians 13:8–13 NIV)

There are various interpretations about what this passage means. I have never found any explanation to be completely satisfactory. However, let me share with you what I think is obvious. Paul tells us there are some spiritual gifts that are temporary, but there are spiritual characteristics that endure for all time.

In 1 Corinthian 12, Paul reveals that every believer has been placed into the Body of Christ by the Spirit. In doing so, the Holy Spirit gave us gifts to serve the greater good of the whole body. He emphasized our gifts are different and uniquely ours. Apparently, and he continues this idea in chapter 14, there were those who thought we should all have the same gifts.

He tells us he wants to "show us a more excellent way." It is the way of love. To demonstrate how superior love is to exercising our spiritual gifts, he tells us how some of those gifts will "cease…be stilled…pass away." On the other hand, "faith, hope, and love" remain. *Do you suppose he is saying that God would still get his work done if only we loved and could do nothing else?*

He says, "Now is the time to grow up!" It is good to know we each have at least one spiritual gift uniquely suited to us. It is great to use those gifts for the benefit of the Body of Christ. But if we go no further than this, we need growing in love.

Paul uses the illustration of how he grew from a child to adulthood. He "talked…thought…and reasoned like a child." As he matured into a man, these were no longer acceptable ways of thinking. Perhaps you have witnessed an adult do something immature and said, "He's so childish!"

I understand Paul to say here that we can work as hard and fervent as our spiritual gifts enable us but still be immature if we do not love. When I seek the applause of men over the applause of heaven, I am being childish. When my labor for Christ seems so burdensome, or unremarkable, or my motives and attitudes lack love, my maturity level is showing.

But! It is a growth process! That's good news! There is no instant spiritual maturity. Paul did not say, "Yesterday I was a child. today, I am an adult." Peter told us to "grow in the grace and knowledge of our Lord and Savior Jesus Christ" (2 Peter 3:18 NIV).

And grow we can and grow we must. Paul ended this amplification of love by telling us what will really endure: "faith, hope, and love." As we mature physically, and as age slows us down, we will find we are no longer able to do what we used to. When doing is no longer possible, we still believe our God, we still rest in his promises, and we still love as he taught us.

The greatest of these is love. When I think about it, one day it will be my turn to leave this world. There is no indication in Scripture that I'll have a Bible study group to teach in heaven. My gifts are left behind. Faith, believing God, gives way to his presence. Hope becomes reality. But love! Blessed, loved! Loving everyone together as we love our God in one accord endures forever and ever!

CHAPTER 37

LOVE IS A WONDERFUL THING

"Love is a wonderful thing," as Michael Bolton sang. It enriches our lives with friends. It brings satisfaction to our hearts and lifelong commitments. There are countless benefits available to us and innumerable experiences of joy that flood into our soul because we love. It is greatly worthwhile. Still, love is costly.

I'm not talking about dollars and cents but the personal investment we make into the lives of those we love. This cost is easily counted in *vulnerability*. When we love, we are opening ourselves to be hurt, maybe devastating pain. We allow ourselves to be impacted by the choices of other people or the events that affect their lives. The examples are abundant, and I am quite sure you have your own list of painful memories.

It is because of this pain we sometimes feel that loving is not worth what we now endure. We hide our hearts away trying to protect it from ever allowing ourselves to be vulnerable again. I've heard some say, "I'll never trust again." "I'll never let anyone get that close to me again." Believe me, please. I've been there. When we hurt so deeply, we build walls between ourselves and any potential threat.

Is love worth it? Is love worth the trauma we experience when our hearts are broken by those we love? Sleepless nights, tear-stained pillows, days of walking in a dark cloud when we experience great loss. Should we hide ourselves away and steel ourselves against being plummeted again?

Great love means great vulnerability, great potential for pain. Let me ask, "Would we want it any other way?" A loved one dies, for whatever reason. We cry out in anguish. tears stream down our face. Need I go on? The greater we love, the greater is the loss and the greater the pain. Would we say we wish we had not loved our spouse, child, or parent?

If our best friend or our mate betrays us, we sometimes are so angry we cannot see past our pain. But shouldn't we hurt? Isn't the joy of love worth the pain? King David knew the joy of friendship and the pain of betrayal. "If an enemy were insulting me, I could endure it; if a foe were rising against me, I could hide. But it is you, a man like myself, my companion, my close friend, with whom I once enjoyed sweet fellowship at the house of God, as we walked about among the worshipers" (Psalms 55:12–14 NIV).

He also shares with us how he dealt with the pain just a few verses later. "Cast your cares on the Lord and he will sustain you; he will never let the righteous be shaken" (verse 22 NIV).

God moved Paul through the Holy Spirit to pen the words of the beautiful love chapter, 1 Corinthians 13. What did he know about that subject? Did he really practice loving others? Did he know anything about the risk of the hurt caused by those he loved?

> Just as a nursing mother cares for her children, so we cared for you. Because we loved you so much, we were delighted to share with you not only the gospel of God but our lives as well. Surely you remember, brothers and sisters, our toil and hardship; we worked night and day in order not to be a burden to anyone while we preached the gospel of God to you. You are witnesses,

> and so is God, of how holy, righteous and blameless we were among you who believed. For you know that we dealt with each of you as a father deals with his own children, encouraging, comforting and urging you to live lives worthy of God, who calls you into his kingdom and glory. (1 Thessalonians 2:7–12 NIV)

> For I wrote you out of great distress and anguish of heart and with many tears, not to grieve you but to let you know the depth of my love for you. (2 Corinthians 2:4 NIV)

> So I will very gladly spend for you everything I have and expend myself as well. If I love you more, will you love me less? (2 Corinthians 12:15 NIV)

> But even if I am being poured out like a drink offering on the sacrifice and service coming from your faith, I am glad and rejoice with all of you. (Philippians 2:17–18 NIV)

Paul, you poured out not only your heart but your body as well because you loved these people so much. Was it worth the pain you felt when they lashed back at you? From the few incidences quoted above, I believe he would say, "Yes, it was worth it. If I had to do it all over again, I would."

Think with me of our Savior. He went to the cross and died for our sins. He rose from the dead. Our sins are paid in full. He did that as the "once for all time" payment so by faith we might share eternal life with him. He did it because he loved us so much.

Yet at times we act as though we do not care when our lives are guided by our human, fleshly nature rather than "Christ's love urging us onward" (2 Corinthians 5:14), personal translation).

His love motivates us into action for the sake of others. Our actions contrary to love are hurtful to our God. "Do not grieve the Holy Spirit of God, with whom you were sealed for the day of redemption" (Ephesians 4:30–31 NIV). "to grieve" means "to cause sorrow." Have you ever thought about our bad choices hurting the Holy Spirit?

Great love produces great joy. It is the ingredient that gives our lives purpose and meaning. The risks are substantial, but the rewards are eternal. Remember, love abides for- ever (1 Corinthians 13:13).

Our God is the source or our love, and our love naturally flows from our relationship with him (1 John 4:7). What will our God do for us when it seems that our love has either backfired or left us shattered in a heap of anguished confusion?

Here's a hint about what we will look at next: "Praise be to the God and Father of our Lord Jesus Christ, the Father of compassion and the God of all comfort" (2 Corinthians 1:3 NIV).

PART 7

GOT ANY QUESTIONS?

CHAPTER 38

WHY?

Why? Sometimes that single word hangs over our heads like a gigantic boulder waiting to drop on us at any moment. As a pastor, Sunday school teacher, and friend, I have listened to that question more times than I can recall.

During my first hospitalization for depression some thirty-five years ago, I met a woman who was also there for the same reason. She had caught her dominant hand in a punch press at work and lost her ring finger and pinkie in less time than it takes to hiccup. She wanted to know, "Why?"

I was absentmindedly listening to her tell her story when she demanded, "Why did this happen to me?" I was too caught up in myself to really care much about what she was saying. I sort of muttered, "I don't know." She became adamant and demanded, "You are a minister! You are supposed to know!"

That is a question for which I have never had an answer. Our standbys aren't adequate. You know them. "God won't give you more than you can handle." "Well, you know God makes all things work together for good." I mustered up sudden ministerial concern to respond, "No, I don't know. But God does!"

It was all she needed to know. She was transformed right before my eyes as she believed God and received peace for her troubled heart. Shortly after this conversation she could leave the hospital and return home with the glow of joy on her face. Sometimes God uses us despite ourselves.

There are answers to those "why?" questions, though they aren't the ones we want to hear. The apostle Paul offers some to us out of his own experiences. By God's grace he had planted a church in city of Corinth. After he left to establish churches in other cities, they wrote him a letter containing questions and circumstances for which they needed his input. His answers are contained in the book of 1 Corinthians.

Paul had to correct several problems and misunderstandings in the church. Some problems were causing divisions and some were disgraceful. He pulled no punches as he tried to bring these believers to a mature walk with the Savior. They did not respond well.

He wrote them a second letter (not 2 Corinthians), which has been lost, to try to resolve the festering conflict. He had his spiritual son, Timothy (1 Corinthians 4:4), deliver the first letter; and the news he brought Paul was not good. Next, he sent Titus, but he was gone longer than Paul had expected. Paul was so troubled he found himself unable to effectively minister the word of God even though he had opened the door of opportunity to him (2 Corinthians 2:13).

> For when we came into Macedonia, we had no rest, but we were harassed at every turn—conflicts on the outside, fears within. But God, who comforts the downcast, comforted us by the coming of Titus, and not only by his coming but also by the comfort you had given him. He told us about your longing for me, your deep sorrow, your ardent concern for me,

> so that my joy was greater than ever. (2 Corinthians 7:5–7 NIV)

Finally, Titus brought the good news to Paul. He was able to reaffirm the love the Corinthians had for Paul. He brought news concerning the work of God's grace in these believers. When Paul wrote 2 Corinthians, he only mentioned one of the problems he addressed in the first letter. Paul was filled with joy and at peace once again.

With this background of what Paul was experiencing at the time of the writing of 2 Corinthians, perhaps we can better understand his approach to that gigantic "why?" question. He had been hurting badly. He was still growing in his relationship with Christ. The apostle who told the Philippian church "be anxious for nothing" (Philippians 4:6 NIV) was worried, anxious, and stressed out!

Here is how he responded to those dearly loved saints in Corinth:

> Praise be to the God and Father of our Lord Jesus Christ, the Father of compassion and the God of all comfort, who comforts us in all our troubles, so that we can comfort those in any trouble with the comfort we ourselves receive from God. For just as we share abundantly in the sufferings of Christ, so also our comfort abounds through Christ. If we are distressed, it is for your comfort and salvation; if we are comforted, it is for your comfort, which produces in you patient endurance of the same sufferings we suffer. And our hope for you is firm, because we know that just as you share in our sufferings, so also you share in our comfort.

> We do not want you to be uninformed, brothers and sisters, about the troubles we experienced in the province of Asia. We were under great pressure, far beyond our ability to endure, so that we despaired of life itself. Indeed, we felt we had received the sentence of death. But this happened that we might not rely on ourselves but on God, who raises the dead. He has delivered us from such a deadly peril, and he will deliver us again. On him we have set our hope that he will continue to deliver us, as you help us by your prayers. Then many will give thanks on our behalf for the gracious favor granted us in answer to the prayers of many. (2 Corinthians 1:3–11 NIV)

He reveals his struggles and despair. It was more than just his concern for them but also the feel of death breathing on him from the circumstances that surrounded him. Please stick around as he gives his perspective on *why* all those distresses fell on him.

CHAPTER 39

COMPASSION AND COMFORT

A dear grandmother had fallen in her kitchen. With a severely broken hip, she lay there in agony for over three days before she was discovered. I was between my junior and senior year in Bible college serving as a summer intern associate pastor. As I visited with her on several occasions, she repeatedly said, "I just don't understand why God would allow me to lay on the floor and suffer that way." I was so naive, I thought I could give her an answer.

When my nephew was suddenly taken from us—he was so young, so full of life, and so dedicated as a servant of the Lord—my question was, "Lord, he was so full of promise. I'm all washed up. Why did you take him? Why didn't you take me instead?"

I'm inclined to believe we all have questions like this from time to time. I don't think that is a bad thing. Even Jesus asked, "My God, My God, why have you forsaken me?" as he was hanging there nailed to the cross (Matthew 27:45 NIV).

As we learned before, God does offer us answers to our "Why?" questions in Paul's second letter to the Corinthians. This letter is the most personal of his writings. He lifts the veil of his circumstance so we can understand that he journeyed a high-risk, peril-filled road.

> We do not want you to be uninformed, brothers and sisters, about the troubles we experienced in the province of Asia. We were under great pressure, far beyond our ability to endure, so that we despaired of life itself. Indeed, we felt we had received the sentence of death. (2 Corinthian 1:8–9 NIV)

He revealed even more in chapter 11.

> [I have been in] prison more frequently, been flogged more severely, and been exposed to death again and again. Five times I received from the Jews the forty lashes minus one. Three times I was beaten with rods, once I was pelted with stones, three times I was shipwrecked, I spent a night and a day in the open sea, I have been constantly on the move. I have been in danger from rivers, in danger from bandits, in danger from my fellow Jews, in danger from Gentiles; in danger in the city, in danger in the country, in danger at sea; and in danger from false believers. I have labored and toiled and have often gone without sleep; I have known hunger and thirst and have often gone without food; I have been cold and naked. Besides everything else, I face daily the pressure of my concern for all the churches. (2 Corinthians 11:23–28 NIV)

Paul shares with us four things he learned through all these trials. First, he said he learned the compassion and comfort of God. "Praise be to the God and Father of our Lord Jesus Christ, the Father of compassion and the God of all comfort, who comforts us in all our troubles" (2 Corinthians 1:3–4 NIV).

God's compassion refers to an emotional response in the ancient Greek language. Have you ever thought of God experiencing feelings? Numerous articles online have identified more than twenty emotional expressions from our Lord Jesus in the gospels. That should be no surprise to us since we are emotional beings created in the image of God.

> For we do not have a high priest who is unable to empathize with our weaknesses, but we have one who has been tempted in every way, just as we are—yet he did not sin. Let us then approach God's throne of grace with confidence, so that we may receive mercy and find grace to help us in our time of need. (Hebrews 4:15–16 NIV)

Simply put, Jesus knows what it is like to be human, to be tempted, to win. He knows what we feel. He feels our pain. Therefore, he can comfort us. He is the one "who comforts us in all our troubles" (verse 4.

The word for *comfort* literally means "to call alongside." It is the name Jesus gave to the Holy Spirit in John 16:7. Picture in your mind a time when you were so tired and weak that your legs felt like rubber. You needed someone beside you to put their arm around you, pull you up tight to himself, and make his strength to become yours.

I literally had that experience before I entered the pastorate as I worked in a factory. I caught three fingers between a pulley and a v-belt on a conveyor. I was screaming in pain as my supervisor ran up and cut the belt. As I stood up, he grabbed me around the shoulders and held me as my knees buckled. I felt like I was almost carried to his car to get me to the ER.

Another way this word can be translated is "encourage or encouragement." As I have learned to trust God, I have felt that kind of comfort from the Holy Spirit more and more with each passing day. Strength, peace, and encouragement have urged me on as my God comes alongside of me to urge me on.

The Holy Spirit has come to dwell in us since the day we believed in Jesus. He is always there as our comforter and encourager. He's always there. Trust him. He will take care of each of us.

CHAPTER 40

WHEN GOD WHISPERS

Our God is so patient and loving. We often rage as we go through the heartbreaks of our lives as we try to figure out what is going on. I am not sure we all fit into Elisabeth Kübler-Ross's categories in her 1969 book *On Death and Dying* (Scribner, a division of Simon and Schuster) as she identified what has come to be known as the Five Stages of Grief.

1. Denial and Isolation
2. Anger
3. Bargaining
4. Depression
5. Acceptance

At one time or another, I can safely say I have experienced these stages, though probably not consecutively or conclusively at one time.

I say that God is patient and loving to us. As we experience this emotional turmoil, often we are trying to deal with our circumstances in our own way, apart from his loving arms. He holds his arms wide open, waiting to embrace us as we work toward acceptance.

Paul called him "the Father of compassion and the God of all comfort, who comforts us in all our troubles" (2 Corinthians 1:3–4 NIV). He is our Father who knows, even experiences, what we feel. He delights to be "called alongside" of us and provide us with his strength in place of our own.

As a father, it occurs to me that I can identify with this concept. I could give a multitude of illustrations gleaned from my years of raising three energetic boys. I hardly know which one to choose, but I'll try.

Our youngest son developed an inguinal hernia at about age five. The surgeon said, "This is no big deal. These little ones bounce back so fast. It is not like us adults." Well, at age twenty-one, I had a hernia repaired; and it was a big, painful deal!

My wife and I were in the surgery waiting area when the doctor told us all went well and we could go in and see our precious little boy. He was just awakening from the anesthesia when we entered the room. He was crying, screaming in pain. We walked over to touch him, speak softly to him, and offer what comfort we could until he drifted back to sleep.

Our hearts were broken. Tears rolled down our cheeks as we held each other. Our thoughts were, *"What do you mean, 'No big deal?' It is a great big deal to us!"* We took him home that day, and surprisingly to us, things went well. The next morning, we went in his room to check on him and ask how he was doing. He threw his blankets back, raised both legs in the air while doing a double kick. Then we understood what the doctor meant.

When Paul was hurting from his circumstances, he found that God is the One "who comforts us in all our troubles" (2 Corinthians 1:4 NIV). *Trouble* is an interesting word. It means literally "pressure, a pressing together." Then by application, it is translated "trouble, tribulation, affliction, persecution, and burdened."

When we are stressed, don't we often say, "I'm under a lot of pressure now." We feel like we are carrying a heavy load, about to be crushed. We may experience all those first four stages of grief, not because of a loss, but because our lives are just not unfolding the way we think they should.

In any, or all of these emotional responses to the events in our lives, God comforts us. He has many ways he can accomplish this in us. Perhaps we stumbled upon or recall a memorized bit of scripture at just the right time. We whisper a prayer of acceptance, and our hearts are flooded with peace. A song of praise can lead our hearts to worship.

It reminds me of the story of Elijah in 1 Kings 18–19. He had witnessed the great display of power as God rained down fire from heaven to consume his waterlogged sacrifice in the presence of the priest of Baal. The challenge was simple: "the god who answers by fire, he is the one true God."

Our God won, but Queen Jezebel reacted badly. She wanted Elijah to pay with his life. Have you ever noticed how people get angry when you reject their position and prove it is wrong? (let's not mention politics and religion!). When we pick up the story next,

> Elijah was afraid and ran for his life. When he came to Beersheba in Judah, he left his servant there, while he himself went a day's journey into the wilderness. He came to a broom bush, sat down under it and prayed that he might die. 'I have had enough, Lord,' he said. 'Take my life; I am no better than my ancestors.' Then he lay down under the bush and fell asleep (1 Kings 19:3–5 NIV).

He was depressed, tired and hungry, not to mention angry.

> All at once an angel touched him and said, "Get up and eat." He looked around, and there by his head was some bread baked over hot coals, and a jar of water. He ate and drank and then lay down again. The angel of the Lord came back a second time and touched him and said, "Get up and eat, for the journey is too much for you." So he got up and ate and drank. Strengthened by that food, he traveled forty days and forty nights until he reached Horeb, the mountain of God. There he went into a cave and spent the night. (1 Kings 19:5–9 NIV)

In verse 10, he is still depressed. He is still complaining about how he is alone, the only servant of God left alive. There is bitterness in his tone. "My nation has rejected you. They've killed all your prophets and now they are seeking to kill me. I give up." Who hasn't uttered words of defeat at one time or another?

> The Lord said, "Go out and stand on the mountain in the presence of the Lord, for the Lord is about to pass by." Then a great and powerful wind tore the mountains apart and shattered the rocks before the Lord, but the Lord was not in the wind. After the wind there was an earthquake, but the Lord was not in the earthquake. After the earthquake came a fire, but the Lord was not in the fire. And after the fire came a gentle whisper. When Elijah heard it, he pulled his cloak over his face and went out and stood at the mouth of the cave. Then a voice said to him, "What are you doing here, Elijah?" (1 Kings 19:11–13 NIV)

A whisper. The whisper of God. He heard every cry of Elijah's heart and answered with a whisper. He wasn't speaking through wind, earthquake, or fire. But God did speak. Elijah again pours out his heart of loneliness and isolation. He felt that after all his sacrifice and service for God, he had been abandoned.

> God comforted his servant in four distinct ways: First—He took care of his physical needs with food, water, and rest. Completely apart from himself, God provided for the needs of his body. Why? He needed it for the journey. We need it too. Too much food and too much rest is not good. *Too much* plays into our depression. Take good note of this. Too many times hurting people have a poor diet and an improper liquid intake resulting in dehydration. Most of us, when we struggle, have poor sleeping habits, either burning the candle at both ends or finding it difficult to get out of bed.

Secondly, he whispered. He reaffirmed Elijah's calling as a prophet. God in essence says, "It's time to get busy again. I'm not done with you yet." In verses 15–17, the Lord gave him some work to do. There were two kings he needed to anoint to succeed to the thrones of Amram and Israel.

Thirdly, he whispered once more. He introduced Elijah to a new friend. God instructed him to anoint Elisha to replace him in his prophetic office. The two were inseparable for the rest of Elijah's life.

Finally, he gently whispered one last time. God gave him a good dose of encouragement. "I reserve seven thousand in Israel—all whose knees have not bowed down to Baal and whose mouths have not kissed him" (1 Kings 19:18 NIV). You are not alone. You never have been.

There was no yelling or screaming. He could have used the wind, the earthquake, or the fire to communicate his message to his servant. He did not. Instead, he whispered.

Elijah was renewed in his spirit because the Father of compassion and the God of all comforts drew him ever so close. He found new strength to walk with God physically, spiritually, and emotionally.

I'm thankful God doesn't yell at me. He's not glaring at me with folded arms and a clenched jaw. He's too busy offering me his comfort and encouragement. He brings refreshment to my soul and a spring of living water. He bids me seek friendship among his servants. And he gives me something to do for his name's sake. All through a whisper.

Let me tell you how it happened. I had come through one of those "black hole" depression experiences when I had wished to die. In the hospital, as I was drifting in and out of consciousness, my wife comforted me with news that God had sold her Florida property for close to asking price in a down real estate market. The financial difficulty we were in was soon to be relieved.

Physically, I grew stronger and was soon able to return to work. That alone was a miracle of God's grace. I had great concern that the prescription drug overdose had caused permanent brain damage. While it took time to recover, my thinking has returned to normal—well as normal as a person with bipolar disorder can be!

Then he gave me a special friend and a ministry all rolled into one. A young couple with kids began attending our Sunday school class. The husband asked me to mentor him as a disciple. We occasionally take breaks, but this mentoring relationship and friendship has been growing for several years now.

No storm. No earthquake. No fire. Just the gentle encouragement of his whisper to keep on keeping on.

God is in the comforting business. It will come gently to us. Quietly. Maybe in a whisper. A friend comes along. Much needed rest and refreshment comes our way. We look around and discover we are not alone. He blesses our service for himself. We find rest and peace in trusting him.

CHAPTER 41

THE VALUE OF A FRIEND

When we ask that hanging question, "Why?" I wonder, what do we really expect for the answer? If we were given a definitive answer, would it satisfy us? Would it be enough? Chances are, if God gave a glimpse into his purposes, we might still be seeking a better response.

It's kind of like the story of a blind man who fell off a cliff and was able to grab hold of a tree limb on the way down. He began screaming for help, and this guy came running to his aid. Seeing the man dangling there was mere inches from the ground, he said, "Just let go!" The fearful blind man asked, "Who are you?" Seeing an opportunity to have a little fun, he said, "God!" The blind man responded, "Is there anyone else up there?"

We really don't want the pat answers we hear during our times of turmoil. I have a few that work for me but probably no one else. It comforts me that even when the questions hang in the air, to be reminded, "this did not take my God by surprise."

It is helpful to me to recognize that God doesn't make the decision to make bad things happen. He allows us and others to act by our own free will as we reap the consequences. Since we live in a fallen world, bad things do and will happen. He allows natural laws to take their own course. Even then, our loving Lord is not the cause of the things that fall on us.

He does not get even with us for our bad choices. Undeniably, we face cause and effect to our actions. By divine decree, what we sow is what we harvest (Galatians 6:7–10). Yet God is not punishing us. God placed all our sins on Christ when he was crucified, and he paid our penalty in full. Nowhere in Scripture do we find that our sins must be punished twice: once by our Savior and then by us when we mess up.

In our pursuit of the elusive "why?" we learned from Paul the Apostle when our heartaches arrive, we can experience the consolation and comfort only God can give. When life pressures us to our breaking point and even beyond, he is there to minister to us in our need (1 Corinthians 1:3–4).

Paul expresses a second outcome of our suffering. Our God is the One "who comforts us in all our troubles, so that we can comfort those in any trouble with the comfort we ourselves receive from God" (2 Corinthians 1:4 NIV).

Our God has created us to need one another. Nowhere is this more evident than when we are hurting. I know many times I have met with people I love who were trying to tough things out in silence and isolation. Some have even denied that there is a problem. But God's grace often prevails to open the door of communication that brings healing.

In verses 5–7, Paul recalls the ministry he had with the Corinthian believers by encouraging them through their suffering the same way God had comforted him and his ministry companions. He told them when they experienced pressure of their problems that he knew how to comfort them because he had experienced the same things.

Who is best able to minister to a parent who has lost a child except another parent who has experienced the same thing? We have special singles ministries in our churches, not to pair them up into couples as much as to lend the support of others who understand the loneliness.

Twelve-step groups seek to encourage others in their fight against addiction by pairing the newly sober individual with someone who has an established sobriety. Why? It is because no one understands the moment-by-moment battle for sobriety like the person who fought the same battles. These groups encourage their people to rely on their "higher power." For the record, my higher power is my Savior, the Lord Jesus Christ.

God has allowed me to teach a Sunday school class for the last eight years. My assignment was to start the class from scratch. When I was asked what I thought the theme of the class might be, I replied, "There are a lot of hurting people. I like to offer some hope to them." Since that day, the class has been known as the Hope Class.

When we are in any trouble, hurting in any way, or needing help, hope, or an encouraging word, it is in those moments that we learn the value of a friend. Who did you call that night you ran out of gas? I didn't have triple A. I called a friend. When I needed someone to share my weaknesses with, I had to search for a friend. When hurts abounded, I had to learn how to be a friend.

One major roadblock we may encounter when we need to be that friend is when we feel obligated to do or to say something. Words are overrated, but the ability to listen is paramount. We may not know what to do, but our greatest ability is availability. It is not waiting to be called but just being there to cry together.

Solomon was the wisest man in the world in his day. I think the only person to ever exceed his wisdom was the Lord Jesus. He penned most of Proverbs, his love song in the Song of Solomon, and his swan in the book of Ecclesiastes, the writings of the Teacher. In his lessons, he gave us good insight into just how important a friend can be.

> Two are better than one, because they have a good return for their labor: If either of them falls down, one can help the other up. But pity anyone who falls and has no one to help them up. Also, if two lie down together, they will keep warm. But how can one keep warm alone? Though one may be over- powered, two can defend themselves. A cord of three strands is not quickly broken. (Ecclesiastes 4:9–12 NIV)

A friend will help us get the job done. Some jobs are just hard to do alone, especially when we are hurting or overwhelmed. A friend recognizes the need and steps in to help. We with bipolar disorder get ourselves in this mess far too often. We can fall apart from anxiety. Our minds race until our hands tremble and it feels like our hearts will burst. A friend will say, "Hey, let me help you." Just a few words and a helping hand can get me back on track.

We may fall, literally, and need a helping hand to get back up. We can fall down a rabbit hole emotionally, or fall flat on our faces morally. The last thing we need is judgment or criticism. A friend, someone to love us unconditionally, can just put their arm around us to allow us to draw on their strength. Solomon well said, "But pity anyone who falls and has no one to help them up."

Nights can be cold when we are alone. You know, those nights when our thoughts race, we toss and turn and can't get comfortable. We're cold and lonely. What we really need is a warm friend to share their warm blanket of love and comfort. Am I comfortable to be around? Do I know how to listen? Can I keep from telling my story until I first hear theirs?

Sometimes I think our pride gets in our way when we think we can fight our battles alone. If we were fighting a literal physical enemy stronger than ourselves, we would welcome the help of a friend. Two friends would be even better. This is true emotionally and spiritually as well. We do not need people to try to fix us but a friend who can be there and say, "Hey, let's get a cup of coffee!" or "Would you like to go fishing [shopping, play golf, or whatever]?"

We fear if we get too close, people can become a drain on us by becoming too demanding. Granted, that can happen, but our God tells us to ask him for wisdom and he will give it generously (James 1:5). This doesn't make for an excuse to not be a friend.

Welcome the friends God sends our way during our troubles, pressures, and stresses. They are his plan for our comfort and are the expression of his compassion. He really is giving us people who hurt with us, who feel our pain.

Now, it is our turn to be a friend and to reach out to others with the same comfort God used to comfort us.

CHAPTER 42

THE VALUE OF A BROKEN FRIEND

Moments after I finished the last chapter, "The Value of a Friend," I opened Facebook and read the following words from a longtime friend. I had first met her and her husband when they joined the first church I pastored. Regrettably, I was hiding many of the same feelings she expresses below. With her permission, I will let her tell her story in her own words.

BROKEN

> The American Heritage dictionary defines "broken" as: shattered… fractured… having been violated… totally subdued… humbled… not functioning… in poor condition… grievously sad. How many times could we Christians say we have felt one or more of these ways?
>
> I spent many years of my adult life feeling all of these things. When people looked at me, they would never have known. I never told anyone. When I looked at the fellow worshippers in the pews, I couldn't understand why they were all so happy. It seemed like somehow, they had the Christian life figured out. They could

pray the most beautiful prayers... they said "AMEN!" at just the right time...they read their Bible every day.

I felt like such a failure as a Christian; I often wondered if I even was a Christian. How could I be a Christian if I was so unhappy... so broken... so sad...in such poor condition? Something was wrong with me.

As I began to look around me in places other than church, I noticed that there were Christians who didn't "have it all together." I worked with Christians who had problems...sadness...brokenness...just as I had. We began to bond as we prayed for each other. We were of different denominations...different upbringings... different races...different doctrines...but the same loving God. They knew Him [sic] just as I knew Him [sic]. I became close to these sisters that shared their struggles with sin...with relationships...with alcohol...with depression...with pain and suffering.

What was it about these relationships that made it possible for me to be open and free to share my deepest struggles? The bigger question was why couldn't I share these struggles at church? In my early years as a Christian, I was in a church and a university that emphasized righteousness and judgment over truth and compassion. When I finally realized the differences, it changed my life. My calling is to be honest about what I am struggling with...honest about my real life...not hiding behind a façade of being perfect. The most important thing I learned: God loves me EXACLY as I am in this EXACT moment.

> Father in heaven, teach me to love. Help me to be honest about my struggles, my failures, my sin, so others may learn about You [sic]. Keep me free from being judgmental and self-righteous. May I become more like you as I grow through each struggle.

Though we live a few hundred miles apart, we've been able to touch base periodically over the past almost forty years. In the beginning, I was as clueless about their pain as they were about mine. Gradually, wounds that could not be hidden any longer became apparent. We allowed each other into our private worlds.

I'll have to admit, without that communication, we could still be suffering in silence. I can safely say, no one, except a very select few, knows my secrets better than this dear couple. There is great value in having this kind of friend.

James validates this kind of relationship. "Therefore confess your sins to each other and pray for each other so that you may be healed. The prayer of a righteous person is powerful and effective" (5:16–17 NIV).

My friend has received about two dozen comments as result of her confession—all positive. So many identified with her feelings and wrote to express their gratitude. I'm sure most of us wish we had learned the value of a friend many years ago.

My earnest desire has been that God's children stop playing church and start being the church. We fear if we shared our faults in church, we would become front page for inner fellowship gossip news. Unfortunately, we cannot trust even church people to love us unconditionally. That's why we need those few close, intimate friends. I have found that if I am vulnerable with people I trust, they will open themselves to me. In that way, we'll benefit.

The Hope Class I am privileged to lead has a motto: "What is said in the class stays in the class." We have some pretty frank admissions when the subject hits a nerve. With the love we have for one another, we do not fear we will be judged by the rest of the class. Still, nothing quite beats sitting down one-on-one and getting to know each other. We share things we don't share with anyone, including our spouse.

I know this has not been a Bible lesson. However, we have learned the application of the previous chapter, "The Value of a Friend." Do you have at least one friend like this? Are we ready to be that kind of friend?

CHAPTER 43

WHEN WE CAN'T RELY ON OURSELVES

After the Blitz by Germany against England, Winston Churchill spoke October 29, 1941, to the Harrow School as things were looking up a bit for Britain. It was in this speech when he sought to impart encouragement and resolve to his beleaguered nation that he gave his famous "Never, never, never, never give up!" speech. Actually, what he said was:

> Never give in. Never give in. Never, never, never, never—in nothing, great or small, large or petty—never give in, except to convictions of honour (sic) and good sense. Never yield to force. Never yield to the apparently overwhelming might of the enemy (*Never Give In! The Best of Winston Churchill's Speeches* [Hachette Books, 2004]).

The apostle Paul gave us two big discoveries he learned during the blitz attacks of the enemy in his life. The first was so he might experience the comfort that only comes from God. Our Lord is the Father of compassion and the God of all comfort. By receiving his comfort, Paul learned how to be a friend and share it with other hurting people.

Now, he shares a third discovery with us. His trials, as dreadful as they were, changed his perspective in life. He learned he could not rely on himself, but he could trust God.

> We do not want you to be uninformed, brothers and sisters, about the troubles we experienced in the province of Asia. We were under great pressure, far beyond our ability to endure, so that we despaired of life itself. Indeed, we felt we had received the sentence of death. But this happened that we might not rely on ourselves but on God, who raises the dead. He has delivered us from such a deadly peril, and he will deliver us again. (2 Corinthians 1:8–10 NIV)

Paul admitted he did not have what it took to be strong and faithful. The situations were beyond his ability to endure. We often misunderstand 1 Corinthians 10:13, "No temptation has overtaken you except what is common to mankind. And God is faithful; he will not let you be tempted beyond what you can bear. But when you are tempted, he will also provide a way out so that you can endure it" (NIV).

Often, we say, "God won't give me more than I can handle!" This verse has to do with temptation to sin. However, circumstance can overwhelm us, so we, like Paul, might learn to not trust ourselves, but rather to lean hard on God. Temptation can be *escaped* by relying on God. Trials, circumstances, are *endured* by relying on God.

It makes me wonder how I could judge anyone who waffles under the pressure of trials. I can look back on many occasions when I really blew it badly. My strength is never sufficient. We can learn a little about this from an experience Christ's disciples endured.

Jesus had been in the process of preparing his disciples for his upcoming arrest, trial, and execution. He knew the days ahead were going to be difficult as he sought to encourage them during his final hours. They weren't getting the message. Instead, they were arguing about which one of them was the greatest! Talk about totally missing the point!

If I were the master, I think I would have wanted to shake them till their teeth rattled to try to get their attention. But Jesus calmly told them they had the wrong perspective. In Luke 22:24–30, He explained the pathway to greatness was in becoming a servant to all.

He then turned to Peter and addressed him pointedly and personally. "Simon, Simon, Satan has asked to sift all of you as wheat. But I have prayed for you, Simon, that your faith may not fail. And when you have turned back, strengthen your brothers" (Luke 22:31–32 NIV).

Peter did not like what he heard the Savior say. "Who *me*?" "But he replied, 'Lord, I am ready to go with you to prison and to death.' Jesus answered, 'I tell you, Peter, before the rooster crows today, you will deny three times that you know me'" (Luke 22:33–34 NIV).

The major point of this passage seems to be our Savior's desire to prepare his disciples, particularly Peter, to never, never, never, never give up! It's going to get tough, so he leads them into the Garden of Gethsemane to pray. Satan wanted to sift them all, especially Peter. They needed to get prepared!

There he will take his closest disciples, Peter, James, and John, off by themselves; and He asks them to pray that they do not succumb to temptation (Luke 22:39–46). But instead of praying, the weakness of their flesh caused them to drift off to sleep, not just once, but three times.

They are all unprepared for what will follow. Jesus will be arrested. Peter will cut off a servant's ear. As the soldiers led him away, the disciples will scatter. Peter will follow at a distance into the temple courtyard. The sifting begins in earnest. Peter is blindsided by his own fears.

Processing wheat was a straightforward step-at-a-time job. First, the grain was harvested, then brought to the threshing floor. There, the heads of wheat were broken apart and the chaff, or outer hull, was broken away from the kernel.

To get the grain separated from the debris, in the cool of the evening when there was a gentle breeze, the farmer would toss the mixture into the air with his winnowing fork. The breeze would carry away the chaff as the grain fell to the floor. This was done repeatedly until the grain lay in a mound and the chaff accumulate into a pile waiting to be burned at the edge of the threshing floor.

This sifting process seems to be a lot like Satan's accusations against Job. "God, you protect him! Take away all he has, take away his health and Job will curse You to Your face!" (Job 1–2). Our God gave permission to the adversary to attack Job with all he could hurl against him short of taking his life. Job was miserable for quite some time but emerged victorious.

In Luke, we discover Satan is again seeking to break down, break apart, and toss around the children of God! In Revelation, he is called "the accuser of our brothers and sisters, who accuses them before our God day and night" (12:10 NIV). He is still active today bringing our names before the throne.

Jesus looks directly at Peter and says, "But I have prayed for you, Simon, that your faith may not fail. And when you have turned back, strengthen your brothers" (22:32 NIV). "Peter, I have prayed for you that you never, never, never, never give up!" Through the process of Satan's attacks to tear him apart, Jesus prayed that Peter's faith would not fail. What about the other disciples? Did Jesus not pray for them as well? That same evening, John 17 records Jesus's prayer for his disciples (verses 6–19). He prayed for divine protection for them (verse 11) and specifically protection from "the evil one" (verse 15). Why was Peter singled out? Perhaps it was because he would be so sifted that his vulnerability would bring him perilously close to giving up.

In that same prayer, Jesus prayed for you and me! "My prayer is not for them alone. I pray also for those who will believe in me through their message" (John 17:20 NIV). He looked down through time and eternity and prayed for us too.

Peter followed from a distance as the soldiers led Jesus away to be tried in an illegal court. Peter decided to hang around, so he warmed himself by the fire. He tried hard to hide among the people. Can you see him attempting to blend in with the crowd? They recognized him anyway. He denied Christ three times, and then something very sobering happened.

> Just as he was speaking, the rooster crowed. The Lord turned and looked straight at Peter. Then Peter remembered the word the Lord had spoken to him: "Before the rooster crows today, you will disown me three times." And he went outside and wept bitterly. (Luke 22:60–62 NIV)

Peter must have felt like he had been hit with the proverbial ton of bricks. He went into the sifter, was broken, and crumbled. Frankly, my friend, that's what the sifter is for. It shows us what we are made of when we walk in our own strength. Peter was sure he could take it. He was wrong. We don't know how long he wept, but he wept bitterly.

Imagine the stab in the heart when his eyes met Jesus's eyes. Imagine the pain in Jesus's heart. Watch Peter as he falls to the ground and buries his face in his arms. Listen to the wailing until the cries become sobs as he gulps for air. Brokenhearted and beaten up, he finds the sifter grinds so slowly.

He existed this way for three days until Sunday morning. The angel told the women at the empty tomb, "But go, tell his disciples and Peter, he is going ahead of you into Galilee. There you will see him, just as he told you" (Mark 16:7 NIV). Make sure Peter gets this message. He's still Christ's disciple, still salvageable after the sifting is over. The chaff has blown away. The wheat remains.

During the ensuing forty days, the resurrected Christ continued to meet with and restore his sifted apostles. They watched him ascend into heaven. A week later, on the day of Pentecost, the Holy Spirit filled the disciple and Peter became the rock on which Jesus promised to build his church (Matthew 16:18). Peter failed the temptation, but his faith did not fail. He never gave up.

Peter never, never, never, never gave up. He came through the sifter. Jesus's prayer was answered. His faith did not fail. Now, through his experience in the sifter, he could strengthen his brothers and sisters in Christ.

What Jesus did for Peter he has done for me. He wants to do the same for all his family. We must all go through the sifter so we may learn not to trust in ourselves but in our God.

CHAPTER 44

IT'S TIME TO PRAY

Ron Hamilton wrote the beautiful song "Rejoice in the Lord." In a very meaningful way, he puts our "Why?" questions into proper perspective. If you have not heard this song preformed, you'll be blessed by checking it out online. The chorus captures the perspective of our "why?" questions in the refrain of this song.

O Rejoice in the Lord
He makes no mistake,
He knoweth the end of each path that I take,
For when I am tried and purified,
I shall come forth as gold

God doesn't make mistakes. He has a plan for everything that happens. Though so much seems to occur haphazardly, we are reminded nothing takes our God by surprise. This is not to say he makes bad things happen. We have free will, and we make our own choices—especially the bad ones. Sometimes we get ourselves into a lot of trouble. Other times we do a lot of good. And sometimes other people make bad choices that affect our lives.

Poor choices can come in the form of mistakes. We make thoughtless decisions and things don't work out so good. It is like the day I took my eyes off the road for just a little too long and looked up in time to see my Impala T-bone a Tahoe SUV. The Tahoe won. One big costly mistake, and I don't even remember what had diverted my attention!

But nothing surprises our God. We have learned that our distresses, those pressure points in our life, allow us to experience the compassion and comfort of our God who loves us unconditionally. Having learned from him what it is like to hurt and then receive his comfort, we in turn offer it to others. The last thing we learned is the pain in our lives teaches us we need his strength to get through these tough patches in our lives. We can't rely on ourselves.

Now Paul shares at least one more blessing that comes out of our dark days. "On him we have set our hope that he will continue to deliver us, as you help us by your prayers. Then many will give thanks on our behalf for the gracious favor granted us in answer to the prayers of many" (2 Corinthians 1:10–11 NIV).

Please! Please never be guilty of saying, "The least I can do is pray." I am not sure why we say that. Maybe it is because we feel we must say something, and a promise to pray sounds spiritual. Prayer is not the least we can do. The least we can do is to do nothing at all!

Prayer is the most we can do. In prayer, we are invoking God's intervention into another person's life. We serve the loving God who declared, "Therefore confess your sins to each other and pray for each other so that you may be healed. The prayer of a righteous person is powerful and effective" (James 5:16–17 NIV). Prayer is his designed plan for getting his will done on earth.

Prayer and thanksgiving are born out of adversity. Specifically, Paul is talking about others praying for him in his trials and, as God answers, his prayer warriors returning thanks to God. Paul is excited that there is such an intimate relationship between him and those he loves so much!

When we have invested ourselves in praying for the specific needs of those we love, we sort of become their cheerleaders as God's answers are revealed. The unfolding of his intervention promotes us to the "praise team" as we offer up our genuine thankfulness for God's answers.

I remember many times when I did not have a vested interest in another person's needs. God answered the prayers, but they were not mine. When the person would come and share with me what God had done for them, I knew I missed a blessing because I had not prayed.

The opposite is also true. My wife prays for me. She knows I discourage easily and I am prone to depression. This week has been a rough week, and I have struggled to write. Today I received a phone call concerning my blog posts on the Internet, which gave me the breath of fresh air I needed. When I called my wife, she rejoiced with me and for me.

Luke, in Acts 12, tells a story about two of the apostles, James the brother of John, and Peter. Both had been taken prisoner by King Herod. James, he had murdered. When he saw that it pleased the religious leaders, he intended on killing Peter as well. He was only waiting until after the Feast of the Passover was over.

"So Peter was kept in prison, but the church was earnestly praying to God for him" (Acts 12:5 NIV). This early church held a special prayer meeting that day. It lasted into the evening hours. It grew dark and bedtime came for even Peter, bound with chains, as he fell asleep in his cell. But the prayer meeting continued.

The night before his public trial was to be held, Peter was sleeping peacefully between two soldiers. I wonder if his ability to sleep was an answer to a prayer for Peter to have peace. An angel appeared with light shining on him as his chains fell off. The angel struck him to wake him up. As they walked through the prison, gates opened by themselves as they passed sixteen soldiers. Peter though he was seeing a vision until he found himself outside, and the angel left him.

> When they had walked the length of one street, suddenly the angel left him. Then Peter came to himself and said, "Now I know without a doubt that the Lord has sent his angel and rescued me from Herod's clutches and from everything the Jewish people were hoping would happen. (Acts 12:10–11 NIV)

At this point, the story almost becomes comical.

> When this had dawned on him, he went to the house of Mary the mother John, also called Mark, where many people had gathered and were praying. Peter knocked at the outer entrance, and a servant named Rhoda came to answer the door. When she recognized Peter's voice, she was so overjoyed she ran back without opening it and exclaimed, 'Peter is at the door!' 'You're out of your mind,' they told her. When she kept insisting that it was so, they said, 'It must be his angel.' But Peter kept on knocking, and when they opened the door and saw him, they were astonished. Peter motioned with his hand for them to be quiet and described how the Lord had him out of prison. (Acts 12:11–17 NIV).

I do not think they doubted God would answer their prayers. They were simply floored by the way God chose. I have been guilty of offering God alternatives as to how my prayer could be answered. Invariably God uses a totally different way I never conceived. It is always better than anything I could dream. He makes it so obvious that he is the one at work in our lives.

Imagine their joy as Peter told the story of the angel, the sleeping guards, gates that opened on their own, and his own realization that this wasn't a dream. It was real! I imagine the praise meeting afterward could have lasted for hours.

This is the whole purpose of prayer requests. It's so easy to treat them lightly, especially if we do not have a closeness or intimate relationship with the people we are asked to pray for. Our challenge is to build relationships that compel us to enter intercessory prayer for each other. The church at Mary's house experienced that relationship with Peter, and they prayed! God answered! Their response is not recorded in this passage, but we know from Acts the church was a praying, praising church.

When we are puzzled about our circumstances, it is okay to ask why. We are certain God has a plan. They are designed to remind us to pray and give thanks to our God.

PART 8

WISDOM FOR OUR DAILY WALK

CHAPTER 45

THE WISDOM WE NEED

It isn't often that I find inspiration from social networking, but I got that and a good chuckle this morning. An unknown Facebook philosopher wrote, "Be decisive. Right or wrong, make a decision. The road of life is paved with flat squirrels who couldn't decide."

To be sure, none of us wants to make bad or wrong decisions. We have reaped too much in the way of consequences to take this matter lightly. Still, someone has suggested, "It easier to direct a moving object than a stationary one."

Honestly, though, sometimes we need direction whether to go metaphorically to the left or right. Sometimes we simply need to know how to stop or refrain from an action or move forward. We want to choose what is right and refuse what is wrong.

What we need is wisdom. The *Oxford Dictionary* defines wisdom as "the quality of having experience, knowledge, and good judgment; the quality of being wise." King Solomon wrote Proverbs specifically to teach wisdom to his son. He starts with an introduction and perhaps the best definition we can find by using several synonyms.

> The proverbs of Solomon son of David, king of Israel:
>
> for gaining wisdom and instruction; for understanding words of insight;

> for receiving instruction in prudent behavior, doing what is right and just and fair;
>
> for giving prudence to those who are simple, knowledge and discretion to the young—
>
> let the wise listen and add to their learning, and let the discerning get guidance—
>
> for understanding proverbs and parables, the sayings and riddles of the wise.
>
> The fear of the Lord is the beginning of knowledge, but fools despise wisdom and instruction. (Proverbs 1:1–7 NIV)

From his opening remarks, we can see wisdom is inclusive of many aspects of life's lessons. An old nineteenth-century English preacher name Charles Haddon Spurgeon perhaps summarized wisdom the best when he wrote, "Wisdom is the right use of knowledge. To know is not to be wise. Many men know a great deal, and are all the greater fools for it. There is no fool so great a fool as a knowing fool. But to know how to use knowledge is to have wisdom" (http:// www.brainyquote.com/quotes/quotes/c/charlesspu121393.html).

Through wisdom we not only recognize the difference between good and bad, valuable and inferior, better and best, just and unfair, we can choose what is right, valuable, best, and fair.

It is apparent that acquiring wisdom is a learning process. There are some people who seem more naturally adept in exercising wisdom. Scripture even speaks of the spiritual gift of wisdom (1 Corinthian 12:8). We are all instructed, however, to ask God for wisdom; and he promises to give it generously (James 1:4). Even Solomon himself asked for wisdom (1 Kings 3:7–13).

God gave Solomon a blank check. "Ask for whatever you want me to give you" (1 Kings 3:5 NIV). He requested wisdom because of his feelings of inadequacy to rule God's people. He felt the weight of his youthfulness. God made him the wisest person to have ever lived. He wrote thousands of songs and proverbs including the biblical books of Proverbs, Song of Solomon, and Ecclesiastes.

In addition, God granted him untold wealth and honor beyond his wildest imagination. His reign was characterized by peace. He was promised long life if he lived obediently as David, his father, had lived.

I find it ironic that even Solomon received wisdom on a learning curve. Though much of it was instant and readily available, he still had room to grow. His wisdom was world renown. Early in his reign he was called upon to make judgments in cases that would have puzzled any other mortal intellect. But…it seems there always has to be a "*but.*" He lacked the wisdom to rule his own spirit.

> King Solomon, however, loved many foreign women besides Pharaoh's daughter—Moabites, Ammonites, Edomites, Sidonians and Hittites. They were from nations about which the Lord had told the Israelites, "You must not intermarry with them, because they will surely turn your hearts after their gods." Nevertheless, Solomon held fast to them in love. He had seven hundred wives of royal birth and three hundred concubines, and his wives led him astray. As Solomon grew old, his wives turned his heart after other gods, and his heart was not fully devoted to the Lord his God, as the heart of David his father had been. He followed Ashtoreth the goddess of the Sidonians, and Molek the detestable god of the Ammonites. So Solomon did evil in the eyes of the Lord; he did not

> follow the Lord completely, as David his father had done. (1 Kings 11:1–6 NIV)

This is a sad commentary on what could have been a glorious reign. When Solomon was old, he reflected on his life and recounted the multitude of ways he tried to find joy in his life. He recorded his thoughts in a diary we call Ecclesiastes. He repeated his conclusions numerous times throughout the book.

He simply said, "The words of the Teacher, son of David, king in Jerusalem: 'Meaningless! Meaningless!' says the Teacher. 'Utterly meaningless! Everything is meaningless'" (Ecclesiastes 1:1–2 NIV). He continued, "I, the Teacher, was king over Israel in Jerusalem. I applied my mind to study and to explore by wisdom all that is done under the heavens. What a heavy burden God has laid on mankind! I have seen all the things that are done under the sun; all of them are meaningless, a chasing after the wind" (verses 12–15 NIV).

We could simply close our Bibles and conclude, "Wisdom isn't worth the effort." We would be wrong. In 11:9–12:1, he lets us know that remembering our Creator from our youth is a good place to start. We will have the opportunity to learn more about how wisdom can affect our attitudes starting with where we are now. I feel encouraged because I know our God is always offering us a new beginning, a new opportunity with each day. After all, I will never be younger than I am today!

> Now all has been heard; here is the conclusion of the matter: Fear God and keep his commandments, for this is the duty of all mankind. For God will bring every deed into judgment, including every hidden thing, whether it is good or evil. (Ecclesiastes 12:13–14 NIV)

Oh, yes, "the fear of the Lord is the beginning of wisdom, and knowledge of the Holy One is understanding" (Proverbs 9:10 NIV). "Do not forsake wisdom, and she will protect you; love her, and she will watch over you. The beginning of wisdom is this: Get wisdom. Though it cost all you have, get understanding" (Proverbs 4:6–7 NIV).

Solomon wasted a life-changing gift by failing to appropriate it to his personal life. I'm not sure how wise I am, but I know what it is like to waste God's gift. The apostle Paul said it is possible to preach effectively and see lives changed only to live an undisciplined life and become "disqualified" (1 Corinthians 9:27 NIV).

Been there. Done that. Got the scars to prove it. I can testify that our God alone can restore the fallen. If wisdom is gained through experience, I guess I've grown a little bit along the way.

CHAPTER 46

DEFINING OUR MISSION STATEMENT

Business organizations formulate a mission statement to clarify to their personnel and customer base the company's guiding principles. The mission statement is written to answer the question, "Why do we do what we do?" The intent is to channel all their activities as a business through the filter of the mission statement.

This is a good idea, not only for organizations but for each of us in our personal lives. Why do we do what we are doing? Let's find a filter that will guide us in eliminating the areas of our lives that are holding us back spiritually. This guiding principle can lead us on to maturity in Christ as we exercise the love he has placed in our hearts.

We could each establish our own governing principles from our own convictions based on the scriptures God places in our hearts. For example, the governing principle to love God above all else and our neighbor as ourselves defines a mission statement that will change our lives forever.

A mission statement can incorporate multiple facets. A manufacturer may first say, "Our mission is to provide superior products at affordable prices. While doing so, we will provide customer service that is superior and satisfactory to our clients."

With that in mind, my personal mission statement contains two aspects. "First, I am committed to love God supremely above all else and to love my neighbor as I love myself. Secondly, I am committed to a relationship with God that governs my behavior by the wisdom he has promised I can have."

Solomon was concerned about his son and wrote specifically to encourage him to seek for wisdom. He issued many warnings against wisdom's antithesis, foolishness. He expounded that following wisdom could even save his life. He encouraged him to use all his strength to acquire this jewel beyond all value.

In the chapter "Wisdom Needed," we discovered several synonyms for *wisdom*: instruction, understanding, insight, prudence, discretion, and knowledge (Proverbs1:1–7). Therefore, wisdom is the accumulation of knowledge gained through experience that directs us into proper decision-making so we may please God. In short, *wisdom is the right use of knowledge.*

When I considered my mission statement, I came to realize that knowing what is right, say, loving one another, and choosing to do what is right are separate entities. For example, as I drive my car down the interstate, I know the speed limit is 65 mph. However, whether I choose to obey that limit or not is a separate choice for me to make. If I choose to ignore it, I may receive a signed invitation to be present in traffic court.

With this in mind, God has provided us with the means by which we can make the right choices in life. It is called wisdom. He wants us to have it. He provides it to us and encourages us to ask him for it. I do not believe God ever made the Christian life to be as difficult as we make it to be. I am convinced that my foolishness muddies my path that causes my own slips, slides, and falls.

It might be good for us to consider for a moment what we can expect wisdom to do for us. If it is truly a guiding principle that will affect our decision-making, let's ask, "What areas of my life will be affected by wisdom?" Solomon gets very specific. He could have said simply that it affects everything, but then I know I would dismiss wisdom as having no real relevance to me.

Wisdom will keep us from falling in with the wrong crowd. "Wisdom will save you from the ways of wicked men, from men whose words are perverse" (Proverbs 2:12 NIV).

When we exercise wisdom, it will keep us from sexual immorality. "Wisdom will save you also from the adulterous woman, from the wayward woman with her seductive words" (Proverbs 2:16 NIV). Remember, Solomon is addressing his son, so the same truths apply to daughters as well.

The person who lives wisely finds a precious treasure that brings not only long life but financial blessing as well.

> Blessed are those who find wisdom, those who gain understanding, for she is more profitable than silver and yields better returns than gold. She is more precious than rubies; nothing you desire can compare with her. Long life is in her right hand; in her left hand are riches and honor. Her ways are pleasant ways, and all her paths are peace. She is a tree of life to those who take hold of her; those who hold her fast will be blessed" (Proverbs 3:13–18).

Have you noticed that wisdom is spoken in the feminine? She will bring honor and recognition to those who possess her. I'm not sure why that is, but perhaps wisdom is something with which Solomon's son needed an intimate, close relationship.

> Get wisdom, get understanding; do not forget my words or turn away from them. Do not forsake wisdom, and she will protect you; love her, and she will watch over you. The beginning of wisdom is this: Get wisdom. Though it cost all you have, get understanding. Cherish her, and she will exalt you; embrace her, and she will honor you. She will give you a garland to grace your head and present you with a glorious crown (Proverbs 4:5–9 NIV).

Do any of us need patience in our lives? Guess how we can come by this rare trait! "A person's wisdom yields patience; it is to one's glory to overlook an offense" (Proverbs 19:11 NIV).

Oh, there is more, much more. I'll mention just one: "The fear of the Lord is the beginning of wisdom, and knowledge of the Holy One is understanding" (Proverbs 9:10 NIV).

It's not a very popular topic, this whole matter of fearing God. It's misunderstood. Downplayed. Minimized. Ignored.

But it sure looks good in a mission statement!

CHAPTER 47

OLD SCHOOL

I was raised old school. My dad and mom simply raised me the way they were raised back during the Great Depression. This affected every area of our lives. Dad was a factory worker, and Mom was a full-time homemaker. I never remember my dad missing a day of work. Finances were tight, and the garden was huge. I learned how to care for the lawn, garden, and livestock on our mini-farm. As the oldest son, that was my job.

Discipline was old school too. I spent what seemed like an eternity sequestered in my room as punishment for my acts of disobedience. To be sure, I misbehaved a lot. There was also the belt on the backside. I know this is considered offensive and even a crime among many in our society, but I am simply telling you how it was back in my day.

All of this did not strike fear into my heart. I can never remember deciding not to do something wrong because I was afraid of my dad. The spankings taught me to hide my disobedience for as long as possible to avoid punishment. I learned how to lie to cover up.

One thing I did learn was *respect.* I did respect my parents. I can only remember back talking to my dad once. I was immediately met with the back of his hand across my face followed with the words, "Do that again, and it won't be the back of my hand!" I was fourteen, and it never happened again. Yet though I respected both of them, it did not keep me from misbehavior.

This same mentality affected my relationship with God for much of my Christian life. As with my parents, I loved him. I respected him, but he seemed so far away, so removed from me. Absent. Though I prayed and studied his Word, preached to other people, taught in small groups, accountability to God seemed so remote.

Solomon teaches us that wisdom will change our perspective in life. Wisdom will cause us to consider consequences to our actions and to direct us to choose what is right. Wisdom allows our relationship with our God to be governed by "the fear of the Lord."

We are introduced to how we can receive wisdom. First, Solomon tells his son to accept his words and store up his commands. "My son, if you accept my words and store up my commands within you…then you will understand the fear of the Lord and find the knowledge of God" (Proverbs 2:1, 5; NIV). We obtain wisdom from wise teachers who instruct us in wisdom. Where does that wisdom come from? "For the Lord gives wisdom; from his mouth come knowledge and understanding" (Proverbs 2:6 NIV).

Secondly, Solomon urges his son to diligently seek wisdom. We are told to turn "your ear to wisdom and applying your heart to understanding—indeed, if you call out for insight and cry aloud for understanding, and if you look for it as for silver and search for it as for hidden treasure" (Proverbs 2:2–4 NIV) the promise made that we will find it.

Do you remember the stories of the California and Yukon gold rushes? Men would sell all they had to move to mountains to dig in the ground or the side of a hill. They waded cold streams to pan for gold nuggets with a dream of striking it rich. Most lost everything. Many died. All but a few went broke. A few became wealthy. All this effort was for the temporary and fleeing hope having a better life.

What kind of effort do we put forward when we are seeking for God's truth, that is, wisdom? He tells us where it comes from. It comes "out of his mouth." When Jesus prayed for his disciples, he said, "Sanctify them by the truth; your word is truth" (John 17:17 NIV).

Wisdom is so much better than the earthly riches we receive from our 9 to 5. When we diligently apply ourselves to gain wisdom, "then you (we) will understand the fear of the Lord and find the knowledge of God" (Proverbs 2:5 NIV).

The huge question is, "What does it mean to fear the Lord?" This is an especially important question when we remember "there is no fear in love. But perfect love drives out fear, because fear has to do with punishment. The one who fears is not made perfect in love" (1 John 4:18 NIV).

Maybe "the fear of the Lord" is one of those old-school things. I don't mean that in a negative sense of being afraid of our God. No, there is a positive way to understand this fear that can profoundly impact the way we perceive him, and in turn, it will change our lives for the better.

As we think of fear, the usual response to a perceived threat is to run away from the thing we fear. For example, my wife is afraid of snakes. Okay, she is *terrified* of the slimy, slithering creatures. She won't even go through the reptile house at the zoo. There are many things that evoke that flight response in us. We are like the armies of Israel as they hid from the booming voice of nine-foot six-inch tall Goliath.

Solomon says wisdom will cause us to "understand the fear of the Lord." I don't think God is encouraging us to shrink back and attempt to hide from him. David confessed, "Where can I go from your Spirit? Where can I flee from your presence?" (Psalms 139:7 NIV). He discovered there was no place to hide.

Often, this fear is referred to as reverence. The *Oxford Dictionary* defines *reverence* as "deep respect for someone." It can even imply a sense of worship. Having a deep respect for our God does not mean that we are afraid of what God may do to us if we step out of line. The fear of the Lord is not a dread that he will hurt us, but rather a fear of what we may do to him. The New Testament tells us two ways we cause pain to our Lord. "And do not grieve the Holy Spirit of God, with whom you were sealed for the day of redemption" (Ephesians 4:30 NIV). And "do not quench the Spirit" (1 Thessalonians 5:19–20 NIV).

The word *grieve* means "to sadden, to distress." My disobedience causes grief, sadness, to the God who loves me and gave his Son for me. *Quench* means literally "to put out a fire." When we resist the Spirit, when we say no to his leading, we are throwing a bucket of water on his holy flame.

Is it any wonder why we feel so powerless in the face of our weaknesses? If we have no reverential awe before him, what will give us incentive to do right? During my years of struggle against my sin nature, I did study the Word and prayed diligently. But I believe I failed to possess the fear of the Lord. I went on sinning with no thought of reverence to my God. I simply pushed forward in my own strength and repeated an endless cycle down.

At this point, I think it is essential for us to be reminded that conducting our lives wisely is a New Testament commandment. "Be very careful, then, how you live—not as unwise but as wise, making the most of every opportunity, because the days are evil. Therefore, do not be foolish, but understand what the Lord's will is. Do not get drunk on wine, which leads to debauchery. Instead, be filled with the Spirit" (Ephesians 5:15–18 NIV).

We live wisely when we are filled with the Holy Spirit. Therefore, we are neither grieving nor quenching him. This is possible when we experience this reverential awe in perception of our God who loves us with an everlasting love.

Wisdom brings us to a right insight of our God. Our view of his majesty will change our lives. Today, when temptation rears its ugly head, I find I must remind myself of the grief my action could bring to my Holy Spirit. You see, we live wisely when our love for him governs the decisions of our lives.

CHAPTER 48

A WISE ATTITUDE

The longer I live, the more I realize the impact of attitude on life.

Attitude, to me, is more important than facts. It is more important than the past, than education, than money, than circumstances, than failures, than successes, than what other people think or say or do. It is more important than appearance, giftedness or skill. It will make or break a company…a church…a home.

The remarkable thing is we have a choice every day regarding the attitude we will embrace for that day. We cannot change our past…we cannot change the fact that people will act in a certain way. We cannot change the inevitable. The only thing we can do is play on the one string we have, and that is our attitude…I am convinced that life is 10% what happens to me and 90% how I react to it.

And so it is with you…we are in charge of our attitudes.

Our attitudes are important. When two people are faced with difficult situations, one may say, "It can't be done!" but the other says, "I think it can." The one who believes it can be accomplished will inevitably be the one who does it.

The apostle Paul told the Philippian church, "I can do all this through him who gives me strength" (Philippians 4:13 NIV). In the context of this passage, he was explaining how he learned the secret to contentment no matter how meager his financial circumstances had become. Attitude made the difference.

Whether we are a success in our walk with Christ or face our days as a continual battle is also a matter of our attitudes. Our spiritual battles are decided by the choices we make. Solomon taught his son, and consequently us as well, that wisdom can direct our attitudes.

The victory comes from within us when we acquire wisdom from its source. We have learned wisdom is the accumulation of knowledge gained through experience that directs us into proper decision-making so we may please God. Again, wisdom is the right use of knowledge. Where can we gain this kind of knowledge that can so permeate our lives as to change us completely?

Solomon compares the acquiring of wisdom to a treasure hunt. Once we have gained her, we are "blessed" or happy. I could use some joy in my life, couldn't you?

> Blessed are those who find wisdom, those who gain understanding, for she is more profitable than silver and yields better returns than gold. She is more precious than rubies; nothing you desire can compare with her. Long life is in her right hand; in her left hand are riches and honor. Her ways are pleasant ways, and who hold her fast will be blessed. (Proverbs 3:13–18 NIV)

I know I am being a little redundant on this subject, but it cannot be overemphasized. "For the Lord gives wisdom; from his mouth come knowledge and understanding" (Proverbs 2:6 NIV). The kind of wisdom you and I need comes out of our relationship with our Lord in fellowship with him in his Word.

Am I seeking him and His Word as a rare treasure, or is my time with him perfunctory, an attitude of boredom? I know every day is not a good day. Some are filled with care, the hours are long, temptations are strong, and we have an overall feeling of exhaustion. There are days when we just have a bad attitude. What are we to do?

Wisdom can guide here too. Every day will not be as things are today, good or bad. God's grace that saved us is the same grace that will navigate us through troubled water. It is a matter of attitude. Will I believe him to do what he has promised to do? If I am wise and believe his Word, I will find his help in my time of need (Hebrews 4:16).

Wisdom guides us to discern between right and wrong. Sometimes we are left with decisions that are differences between better and best, or two equally good choices. How do we know what to do? Wisdom, that attitude of trusting God in all things, makes the difference. "Trust in the Lord with all your heart and lean not on your own understanding; in all your ways submit to him, and he will make your paths straight" (Proverbs 3:5–6 NIV).

> Blessed is the one who does not walk in step with the wicked or stand in the way that sinners take or sit in the company of mockers, but whose delight is in the law of the Lord, and who meditates on his law day and night. That person is like a tree planted by streams of water, which yields its fruit in season and whose leaf does not wither—whatever they do prospers. (Psalms 1:1–3 NIV)

This very happy person is walking wisely in the delight of God's Word. He has found the guiding influence of his life, and it affects the way he behaves in a very ungodly environment. And he is blessed. The word means "happy," and it is a plural exclamation, "Oh, the happinesses!" That may not be good grammar, but maybe we can get the idea of how much joy is waiting for those who walk wisely in this life.

What is it like when we make the wise choice? "Now then, my children, listen to me; blessed are those who keep my ways. Listen to my instruction and be wise; do not disregard it. Blessed are those who listen to me, watching daily at my doors, waiting at my doorway. For those who find me find life and receive favor from the Lord. But those who fail to find me harm themselves; all who hate me love death" (Proverbs 8:32–36 NIV).

Perhaps we have agonized over a decision and maybe chose the one we believed to be best, not because we wanted it but because wisdom moved us in that direction. We sur- render our will; in an attitude of acceptance, we chose the wise path. In a short while, joy fills our hearts because we know we are right.

A couple of years ago, we had to buy another car. In the past, car buying was an impulsive experience for me. I usually would buy a new car or a very recent model and end up in debt for a long time. At about the third month, I would already be sick of car payments.

This last time, we had an insurance settlement check from my Impala I had totaled. The check was generous, and we prayed to find a good used car that we could pay for without a loan. When the dealerships saw the sum of money we had, they saw dollar signs! "Great down payment you got there! We can put you in a brand-new car!" No, thanks!

I'll shorten the story, though it really got kind of funny. We ended up at a dealership talking to a sales manager who is a friend of my wife's son. He put us in an extra-clean, well-maintained SUV—tax, title out the door with a thousand dollars left over! It is more than we hoped for with fewer miles and a year newer. Wisdom rewarded us with the joy of trusting God.

What can wisdom do for me in my hours of temptation? I used to think, "I'm just going to fight this temptation until I'm totally stressed out, and then I'll give in. I might as well go ahead and do it now." What a defeated attitude!

A positive attitude says, "No temptation has overtaken you except what is common to mankind. And God is faithful. He will not let you be tempted beyond what you can bear. But when you are tempted, he will also provide a way out so that you can endure it" (1 Corinthians 10:13 NIV).

Wisdom believes there is a way to escape. Wisdom searches for the way out even if we fail. Wisdom helps us get back up. Wisdom finds the way out.

Our situations are never hopeless. Jesus promised, "You will know the truth, and the truth will set you free" (John 8:32 NIV). Wisdom comes out of the mouth of our Lord.

CHAPTER 49

UGH! CRITICISM!

I believe God has a sense of humor. He waits until just the right time, and then *bam!* here is a lesson we didn't know we needed to learn! I think he gets a chuckle out of his perfect timing. This chapter is one of those times. You see, I have a problem accepting criticism. So, as I have meditated and studied, *bam!*

Throughout our lives, we have had to face those who seek to correct us. I think, mostly, people love us and mean well, but it doesn't necessarily make their words any easier to accept. Such is my case as I have worked on this chapter over the last several days.

My wife loves me dearly, and she understands me better at times than I wish she did. A person with bipolar disorder is subject to two extremes. One, obviously, is depression. The other is mania, or "periods of great excitement, euphoria, delusions, irritability, and over activity" (*Oxford Dictionary*). As such, I can become singularly directed to the exclusion of other activities.

She understands my passions but tries to get me to see the importance of managing my activities to do other important things along with my drive to study and write. It balances me out and helps to keep me from anxiety and stress. It takes a big man to say, "Honey, you are right." Yesterday, I was not a big man!

I come from a proud heritage of stubborn men. I resent being told what to do. Even in my employment history, I resented my boss telling me to do what I clearly understood my responsibilities to be. So, you can imagine, yesterday was a not-so-pleasant day of stubborn resentment. What really put the icing on the cake was my wife, Pam, thought my stubbornness was funny! Throw some gasoline on that fire over there, boys!

This lesson is for me. A wise person accepts reproof, or criticism. "Do not rebuke mockers or they will hate you; rebuke the wise and they will love you. Instruct the wise and they will be wiser still; teach the righteous and they will add to their learning" (Proverbs 9:8–9 NIV). A wise man not only accepts the rebuke, but they will love you for it as well. I'm a little slow on the acceptance end.

The first thing we need to do is consider the source. "Faithful are the wounds of a friend, but deceitful are the kisses of an enemy" (Proverbs 27:6, NASB). "Let a righteous man strike me—that is a kindness; let him rebuke me—that is oil on my head. My head will not refuse it, for my prayer will still be against the deeds of evildoers" (Psalm 141:5 NIV).

We can trust the people who love us to tell us the truth. "As iron sharpens iron, so one person sharpens another" (Proverbs 27:17 NIV). We have blind spots in our lives. Since we cannot see them, God provides us with friends and loved ones to help open our eyes.

What do we do when we are unjustly criticized by hateful people? Let me tell you, lashing back or storming off does not work, though I admit that is my first inclination. From personal experience, I can say that defending myself is seldom useful because the other person is not likely to understand or listen to what I'm trying to say. It usually degrades into trading verbal punches. As our discussion degenerates into an argument, we don't even listen to what the other person is saying because we are too busy thinking about what we will say next. It is all so unproductive.

Something I try to do, at least that is until yesterday, is to pray, calm down, then look for the kernel of truth hidden behind the painful rhetoric. Regardless of the source, "instruct the wise and they will be wiser still; teach the righteous and they will add to their learning" (Proverbs 9:9 NIV).

Why is it so hard to accept criticism even from those who care deeply for us? "When pride comes, then comes disgrace, but with humility comes wisdom" (Proverbs 11:2 NIV). One of the hardest lessons we have to learn is saying those three words: "I was wrong." Our proud hearts refuse to acknowledge that someone else may be right.

"A rebuke impresses a discerning person more than a hundred lashes a fool" (Proverbs 17:10 NIV). The contrast here is striking. A wise person benefits from rebuke. He is impressed to the point of making changes in his life. A fool can be beaten with a hundred lashes and still not benefit from the rebuke. He keeps doing the same thing over again.

The following are verses from Proverbs that instruct us concerning the value of accepting criticism. May the source be family, friend, or foe, we can humbly accept the criticism for what it is worth. As long as we are in this life, correction will be needed. It may be painful. It can be beneficial even if it is unfair, unwarranted, or unkind.

> Whoever heeds life-giving correction will be at home among the wise. (15:31 NIV)

> Like an earring of gold or an ornament of fine gold is the rebuke of a wise judge to a listening ear. (25:12 NIV)

> Listen to advice and accept discipline, and at the end you will be counted among the wise. (19:20 NIV)
>
> Whoever heeds discipline shows the way to life, but whoever ignores correction leads others astray. (10:17 NIV)

I should add that when we offer reproof or criticism, we should be very well certain that what we have to offer is genuinely necessary to be said. "Instead, speaking the truth in love…Do not let any unwholesome talk come out of your mouths, but only what is helpful for building others up according to their needs, that it may benefit those who listen" (Ephesians 4:15, 29 NIV).

I am of the conviction that if I am to speak to someone about an area of their life that needs correcting, God will impress me with fitting words to say at the right moment in time. Otherwise, I must wisely remain silent. "Like apples of gold in settings of silver Is a word spoken in right circumstances" (Proverbs 25:11 NIV).

God has never called us to be judges. We all know John 3:16, but do we know verse 17? "For God did not send the Son into the world to judge the world, but that the world might be saved through Him" (NASB). If Jesus did not come into this world to judge, then we ought not think it is our job to do it!

We are not called to be critics. There is no such thing as the gift of criticism. When we must reprove or correct someone, we must prayerfully, carefully do it by the leading of the Holy Spirit.

If we are wise, we will welcome it. Now, I have to plan what to say to my wife when she comes in tonight.

CHAPTER 50

WISDOM: GUARDING OUR INTEGRITY

Solomon teaches his son many lessons about doing the right thing, making the right choices, and guarding his heart from the painful consequences of foolish living. "Watch over your heart with all diligence, For from it flow the springs of life" (Proverbs 4:23 NIV).

I really wish I could point to Solomon's life and show how wisdom saved him from the pitfalls of life, but I cannot. I also wish I could point to his son, Rehoboam, and demonstrate by his example that he followed his father's instructions, but, again, it is not possible.

More than anything, I wish I could tell you how I became wise and avoided behavior that had dire consequences, but, as before, to do so would not be the truth. What I can say to all of us is simply this: Wisdom keeps its promises when we pursue it as God has instructed us to.

Proverbs has meaning to those of us who desire to be wise. Without the drive to acquire wisdom, all Solomon's instructions, warnings, and admonition are wasted. We will not listen or heed the truth if our heart is bent on having our own way. "The fear of the Lord is the beginning of knowledge, but fools despise wisdom and instruction" (Proverbs 1:7 NIV).

Integrity is the issue at stake. A person of integrity has the quality of being honest and having strong moral principles. Without integrity, we are slaves to our own passions. In Solomon's words, we are fools. "A fool finds pleasure in wicked schemes, but a person of understanding delights in wisdom" (Proverbs 10:23 NIV). "Whoever walks in integrity walks securely, but whoever takes crooked paths will be found out" (10:9 NIV).

Charles Swindoll said it this way:

> Integrity is completeness or soundness. You have integrity if you complete a job even when no one is looking. You have integrity if you keep your word even when no one checks up on you. You have integrity if you keep your promises. Integrity means the absence of duplicity and is the opposite of hypocrisy. If you are a person of integrity, you will do what you say. What you declare, you will do your best to be. Integrity also includes financial accountability, personal reliability, and private purity. A person with integrity does not manipulate others. He or she is not prone to arrogance or self-praise. Integrity even invites constructive and necessary criticism because it applauds accountability. It's sound. It's solid. It's complete. (Charles R. Swindoll, "A Battle for Integrity," *Insights* (March 2003): 1–2)

There are things from my past I hate to admit. I have been a fool, despising wisdom and loving my sin more than I loved my Savior. The encouragement I can give to every- one is, "It doesn't have to stay that way." "How can a young person stay on the path of purity? By living according to your word. I seek you with all my heart; do not let me stray from your commands. I have hidden your word in my heart that I might not sin against you" (Psalm 119:9–11 NIV).

You see, integrity is the way of wisdom. It all begins with a decision to walk with Christ and seek his face. We can search for wisdom in the pages of his Word and the godly people he brings into our lives. Admittedly, in the beginning, we may need dozens of restarts in a week. We need commitment to never give up on this pursuit of wisdom. We need integrity.

Listen to Wisdom's rebuke as she speaks, "Out in the open wisdom calls aloud, she raises her voice in the public square; on top of the wall she cries out, at the city gate she makes her speech: 'How long will you who are simple love your simple ways? How long will mockers delight in mockery and fools hate knowledge? Repent at my rebuke! Then I will pour out my thoughts to you, I will make known to you my teachings'" (Proverbs 1:20–23 NIV).

Here is Wisdom speaking to those who lack her: "Wisdom has built her house; she has set up its seven pillars. She has prepared her meat and mixed her wine; she has also set her table. She has sent out her servants, and she calls from the highest point of the city, 'Let all who are simple come to my house!' To those who have no sense she says, 'Come, eat my food and drink the wine I have mixed. Leave your simple ways and you will live; walk in the way of insight'" (9:1–6 NIV).

In chapter 8, verses 22–30, Wisdom declares she has existed since before man was ever created. She has experience, knowledge, and instruction to pass on to us. As we read in chapter 9, she has prepared a banquet table for us. Her invitation is broad. Everyone is invited to join her around her table. All who are simple; lacking understanding, discernment, knowledge; or who are caught up in "simple" unwise lifestyles are invited.

The beauty is, no matter where we are or what we find ourselves caught up in, it is not too late! Wisdom is crying out to you and me to sit down at her banquet table, eat bountifully of her words and drink deeply of her wine of knowledge. We can return anytime we need a refill. The table is always spread, and she is ready to grant us our need.

What obstacle lies in your way today that hinders your walk with Jesus? I want us to be gut-level honest with each other today. Each of us struggle in our own private world. There is no room for judgment simply because someone may sin differently than I do. Whatever it may be, we have hope. Remember, we are given the directive to walk wisely, know God's will, and be filled with the Holy Spirit (Ephesians 5:15–18). That is integrity in progress.

A wise person will recognize where they are and accept correction. "Whoever loves discipline loves knowledge, but whoever hates correction is stupid" (Proverbs 12:1 NIV). "Whoever heeds life-giving correction will be at home among the wise" (15:31 NIV). When we accept correction, we begin our journey in wisdom. Our course corrections place our feet on the road of integrity.

Whatever our moral failures may be, God desires to change us. I wish I could give each of us three Bible verses and a prayer to overcome whatever failure have plagued us in the past. The truth of the matter is simply this: there are no quick and easy fixes. As much as I have sought instant cures for my sinful habits in the past, victory has been found only through faith and a close walk with Jesus. Integrity comes when we sit down at Wisdom's table and search for her with all our heart.

PART 9

CHRISTMAS MEDITATIONS

CHAPTER 51

MARY, DID YOU KNOW?

By our standards today, Mary was just a girl barely in her teens, too young for marriage, and definitely too young to have a baby. As we would expect, she is a virgin, and she is troubled by the message of an angel sent to give her a life-altering assignment.

"'Greetings, you who are highly favored! The Lord is with you.' Mary was greatly troubled at his words and wondered what kind of greeting this might be. But the angel said to her, 'Do not be afraid, Mary; you have found favor with God'" (Luke 1:28–30 NIV). Simply stated, she is told, "Mary, I've got great news for you! God's grace is on you!"

She might have thought, "*Just what is this guy talking about?*"

"You're about to become a mommy! You'll have a boy who is God's son. You will name him Jesus, and he will sit on his grandfather David's throne to rule over all Israel!" (verses 31–34). Can you imagine how her mind is reeling?

I'm a virgin! How can I have a baby? My marriage to Joseph is months away. How can this be?

"The angel answered, 'The Holy Spirit will come on you, and the power of the Most High will overshadow you. So the holy one to be born will be called the Son of God'" (Luke 1:35 NIV).

"Mary, this is a miracle—a God thing. Your child will be the Son of God."

"'I am the Lord's servant,' Mary answered. 'May your word to me be fulfilled.' Then the angel left her" (verse 38 NIV). Personally, I believe this statement of faith expressed by Mary marked the moment of conception of our Savior in her womb.

"Mary, did you know?" the question raised by songwriter, Mark Lowery, stirs our hearts. Think with me for a moment about what happened in that instant. Something changed in heaven and on earth in that single instant. God is the eternal Triune God who has always existed as the Father, Son, and Holy Spirit. We can trace these three Persons through the pages of scripture from eternity past to eternity future. We can catalogue and define their attributes and discover that all three are equal.

So, I ask, "What happened at that moment of conception to the Second Person of the Godhead?"

> Have this attitude in yourselves which was also in Christ Jesus, who, although He existed in the form of God, did not regard equality with God a thing to be grasped, but emptied Himself, taking the form of a bond-servant, and being made in the likeness of men. Being found in appearance as a man, He humbled Himself by becoming obedient to the point of death, even death on a cross. (Philippians 2:5–8, NASB)

How does God become a man? He empties himself. He voluntarily lays aside his equality and submits himself to the will of the Father. Instead of divine characteristics, He takes on the form of a servant. He takes, through the virgin birth, human form. Because he took on humanity, he accepts death on the cross for the punishment of our sins. Though he retained his identity as God, he surrendered the full use of his divine attributes.

Let's let our minds go wild for a few minutes. Imagine God, who "though he was rich, yet for your sake he became poor, so that you through his poverty might become rich" (1 Corinthians 10:9 NIV). Imagine, He did this as a gift to us. ("For you know the grace of our Lord Jesus Christ.")

And for you and me, he took on the poverty of humanity in order to share with us the riches of eternal life. But what form did that poverty take?

At that moment of conception, heaven has changed. The Son no longer sat at the right hand of the Father. Where is He? He has limited himself to a single fertilized cell in the womb of a young virgin. There, for nine months he will grow. He will experience all an unborn-child experiences. His heart will experience its first beat. Mary will feel his first kick.

When the day to be born arrives, his body feels the contractions as his head presses toward the birth canal. He takes his first breath. He has a startled response when he finds no restraint to his first stretch. Mary puts diapers on the Son of God. He cries if he's cold or hungry. He must learn to crawl and then to walk and to talk.

He is as much human as is his mother and as much God as is his Father. As a human, he became so tired he was sleeping through a storm while he rode in a boat. He was hungry, so he sought fruit on a fig tree. He agonized and cried as he prayed the night He was arrested.

> "During the days of Jesus' life on earth, he offered up prayers and petitions with fervent cries and tears to the one who could save him from death, and he was heard because of his reverent submission. Son though he was, he learned obedience from what he suffered and,

> once made perfect, he became the source of eternal salvation for all who obey him" (Hebrews 5:7–9 NIV).

So why did God go through all this? "And being found in appearance as a man, he humbled himself by becoming obedient to death—even death on a cross!" (Philippians 2:8 NIV). It was for you and me. It was so he could die for us. "The wages of sin is death" (Romans 6:23). So, he paid our debt. I can't pay your debt because I could only pay my own. If I did, my debt would never end because I would receive the penalty of eternal death.

"Since the children have flesh and blood, he too shared in their humanity so that by his death he might break the power of him who holds the power of death—that is, the devil" (Hebrews 2:14 NIV). Through his death and resurrection (1 Corinthians 15), Jesus dealt completely with our sin problem.

Mary raised her baby boy through his infancy, as a toddler, and through his childhood into adolescence and adult- hood. Did he fall and scrape his knee? Did he love to be held and cuddled? Was he just a normal kid who loved to play peekaboo and play tricks on his younger half brothers and sisters? All of this, and he never sinned!

Mary, did you ever forget who you were raising? You had a momentary lapse when he was twelve and you referred to Joseph as his father. Did you worry that day he left to begin his ministry? How did you feel as you watched your hometown attempt to stone him? What was it like when you saw all your younger sons say he was crazy?

Mary, you were there at Calvary. You were so alone, from the cross he commissioned the apostle John to take care of you. You watched him bleed and die. You heard what he had to say, but did you realize this day was really going to come?

We celebrate Christmas as the birthday of our Savior. His birth explains to us why his death on the cross and his resurrection could take away our sins. He is God Who became man to live without sin and pay our eternal penalty. Through all this, he offers the gift of eternal life to all who believe in him.

But the story is not over. "Therefore God exalted him to the highest place and gave him the name that is above every name, that at the name of Jesus every knee should bow, in heaven and on earth and under the earth, and every tongue acknowledge that Jesus Christ is Lord, to the glory of God the Father" (Philippians 2:9–11 NIV).

I would rather bow my knees to him now than to wait until eternity. Jesus, you are my Lord!

CHAPTER 52

THE GUIDING STAR

There it was. It was a bumper sticker on the car in front of me. I can't remember the last time I had any kind of saying plastered on my car, but I really liked this one: Wise Men Still Seek Him.

I've thought a lot about those brief words through the years and not just at Christmastime. I really think my story is more about him seeking me than it is about me seeking him. Nevertheless, this story in the Bible is about a guiding star that led a small group of men to see baby Jesus.

I suppose there were three men, though I don't know. The account in Matthew 2 says only that there were more than one and they brought three gifts: gold, frankincense, and myrrh. We do know they came from the east, probably across the Fertile Crescent from ancient Persia. It was a journey that would take months.

Who were they? Folklore has embellished the story, so let's just stay as close to Scripture as we can. The NIV tells the story this way: "After Jesus was born in Bethlehem in Judea, during the time of King Herod, Magi from the east came to Jerusalem and asked, 'Where is the one who has been born king of the Jews? We saw his star when it rose and have come to worship him'" Mathew 2:1–3. I wonder if they were astonished when they discovered no one had a clue what they were talking about.

The KJV calls them wise men. *Magi* is really an untranslated Greek word. Our understanding of who they were goes back to Daniel. Daniel was a member of Babylonian and Persian royal court advisors known as wise men, magicians, and astrologers the king was going to execute until Daniel stepped forward (Daniel 2).

Daniel wrote his prophecies while in Babylon, and from Daniel 9:2, we know Jeremiah's writings were available there. It appears his influence was not only widespread in his day but long-reaching beyond his lifetime. I don't think it is too outlandish to think that the men were greatly influenced by the Jewish God Daniel so fervently served.

Here is what we know: They saw a star. The star was significant because it belonged to One who was born King of the Jews. They came to worship him and give gifts to him. This may indicate they believed him to be move than human, even divine as they desired to worship the child. The message they brought concerning their mission troubled King Herod, the religious leaders, and the whole city of Jerusalem.

Let's focus on the star the wise men saw. If I understand Matthew correctly, the star appeared long enough to indicate a very special event occurring somewhere to the west. How long it appeared, no one knows. The star wasn't visible when they arrived in Jerusalem. Apparently, no one else had noticed the star when it first appeared.

But when they came, they came with purpose. Did they dig through the scrolls left by Daniel, Jeremiah, and those Jews who might have lived a long time ago in Mesopotamia? At any rate, they knew the King of the Jews had been born. They studied. They packed up and put together a caravan. They traveled hundreds of miles following the trade routes.

It's been months by the time they arrive in Jerusalem. Imagine, they've gone through all this with great expectations, and no one knows what they are talking about! The religious leaders had to go look it up! And even at that, those leaders were not interested enough to go check it out for themselves.

As they left the city on their way to Bethlehem, the star reappears to lead them, not to a manger, but to the house where Mary, Joseph, and Jesus were then living (Matthew 2:9). Amazingly, these wise men are the only people affected by the starlight that beckoned them to follow until it stopped over the house. No crowd. No entourage. Just these Gentile foreigners.

Think about your star. You know, the one who brought you to Christ or perhaps a closer walk with the Savior. What happened meant something special to you, but maybe it skipped over the head of others. You, maybe a few others, were simply changed forever because of the guiding star God sent your way.

I received Christ as my Savior in my teens; I was miserable. I didn't know my church's entire youth group, as well as my family was praying for me. Our church was an old-time country-style Baptist church from the mountains of eastern Kentucky. One of the preachers asked me one Sunday morning how I was doing. I replied, "Not so good." He knew what I meant, and I watched his heart break as I looked at his face.

He preached that morning. I have no idea what it was about, but during the altar call, he loudly shouted, "There is a young man here I want to see saved!" Sitting in the back row, I had no doubt about who he was referring to. It was the hardest thing I had ever done, but I stepped out of my row and walked down the aisle. I received Christ that day.

In later life, I would again need a star to guide me back to a close walk with Christ. I could name several individuals, but I cannot comprehend the number of people who, behind the scene, prayed for me. I think I can say my church, Parkview United Methodist in Miamisburg, Ohio, was my guiding star.

At Christmas, we recall so many memories of family, friends, and celebrations of our Savior's birth. When we gaze on the Christmas star and the wise men, let's take a moment to give thanks for those who guided us to Christ. These dear ones have made it possible for us to say, "Jesus is the reason for the season" as well as every day of our lives.

PART 10

SOMETHING TO THINK ABOUT

CHAPTER 53

SOMETHING FOR GUYS TO THINK ABOUT (AND LADIES WHO CARE HOW MEN THINK)

Guys, we all struggle with lust even if we think we have it hidden. An old sage once said, "All men struggle with lust. Those who say they don't are either dead, dying, or lying!" One book is even titled *Every Man's Battle (*.

No, men don't have monopoly on the subject of lust. Women have their own set of problems. Otherwise, *Fifty Shades of Grey* would have never become a best seller, romance novels would only sparsely populate the super-market bookshelves, women's magazines would go out of circulation, and soap operas would be all washed up.

But I'm writing to guys. Specifically, I'm writing to Christian men who sincerely want to walk with Jesus. We are aware of the scripture that tell us that to lust after a woman not our wife is to commit adultery in our hearts. Right now, we don't need another message of condemnation about a behavior concerning which we already carry so much guilt and over which we feel so powerless.

I have two thoughts I'd want to share. First, quit blaming the women. I know, and I hear you. Why do women dress so sexy? It has been pointed out to me that even in church, young women and mature ladies dress in ways that make our self-restraint difficult. I agree. It happens.

Guess what? I am not responsible for how any woman dresses! What I am responsible for is my reaction. I wish Christian women would make my job easier. But if they don't and I lust, who is responsible? Me, that's who!

Anything can provoke lust: dress that reveals too much while standing or bending over, an inappropriately warm hug, standing too close, lingering touches, a brush or pressing of a breast against the arm, etc. You know what I am talking about, and any of these incidents can send us guys into lust overdrive.

You know, I don't care why these things happen. For me to dwell on them in my thoughts is to be lustfully intoxicated. I must take care of me and let God take care of the women. Remember, only he can change a person's heart. I am not about to pronounce condemnation upon my sisters in Christ. Do they know how we men respond to sexy dress and provocative actions? I do not know! What I do know is the only person I am responsible for is me. Actually, Titus 2:3–5 gives the responsibility of teaching younger women about these things to the senior women of the congregation.

Preventively, I've learned to anticipate triggers. Like Job of old, "I made a covenant with my eyes not to look lustfully at a young woman" (Job 31:1 NIV). We can learn to focus our eyes elsewhere rather than follow through with a lustful look. For me it often means shifting my stance in such a way as to be unable to gain a direct look. If there is an inappropriate touch, stepping away communicates that the contact is not wanted.

Actively, I need a pressure release valve in my life, someone I can tell exactly what happened and what I felt. For me, that person is my wife. She is not the jealous type and knows that this is my way of releasing the emotions provoked by lust. I think it would be a huge mistake to assume your wife can handle this. Clear it with her first. You may need to find a man you can trust who can serve as your pressure release.

The second thing I have found helpful is accepting myself as a forgiven child of God. He made me with the capacity to experience passion. His design grants fulfillment in marriage to my wife. Any expression of my sexuality outside of marriage is forgiven through the completed work of Christ.

Guilt is a chain that binds me to lust. A lapse in discipline concerning lust can quickly be dealt with by confessing it to the Father (1 John 1:9). Yet if I allow thoughts of guilt like, "*How could I have done that, again? I'm a failure!*" invade my thinking, my shame and rehashing of history will set me up to fail again.

Do I still struggle? Well of course! Things are better now, but I must be on my guard. Paul, in Romans 7, shared his own battle with the flesh. He concluded victory was possible through Christ (7:25). Listen to these words of encouragement: "Therefore, there is now no condemnation for those who are in Christ Jesus" (Romans 8:1 NIV). If I fall, he doesn't condemn me. I must not condemn myself.

CHAPTER 54

MY POLITICALLY INCORRECT THEOLOGY: ARE THE LOST REALLY LOST?

The buzzword for the past four decades or so demands that we be "politically correct" in both our vocabulary and our positions or beliefs. I'll have to admit I've had a lot of fun with the vocabulary part.

It all started back in the seventies when I had a load of miscellaneous castoffs that was too large for the garbage man—oops, sanitation engineer—to carry away. I called the local government office and asked where the "city dump" was. The lady on the other end said, "Sir, do you mean the County Sanitary Landfill?" Me, "Yeah! Close enough!"

People we once called airheads are now *pneuma-cranial.* That lazy person at work has "motivation deficit disorder." When we make an obvious blunder, or forget something simple, we no longer need to use crude terms, for it can now know it is "a flatulent of the inner cranial nerve tissue!"

Change has been good in many respects. Terms that demean race or gender are now taboo, though some are slow in getting the message. Hopefully, stereotypical language will continue to fall into disuse.

There are some subjects in which I will always be "politically incorrect." For me, I'll always say "Merry Christmas!" and "God bless you!" I will continue to respect the flag of our country by standing, facing the flag, and covering my heart with my right hand when "The Star-Spangled Banner" is played. I wish our students were still taught to say the pledge of allegiance to the flag.

Unfortunately, the church of our Lord Jesus Christ has become infected with a virus of political correctness along with society. I've noticed there are subjects that are seldom addressed in Christian culture anymore—subjects like sin in general and sexual immorality specifically, Satan, and hell.

There seems to be an acceptance of all creeds and a belief that truth is flexible; for example: your truth is as valid as mine. We all go to heaven because God is a god of love, and a loving God could send no one to hell.

To be honest, I wish it were true that everyone goes to heaven. I would really like to believe that. It makes me sad to think of anyone going to hell, especially those I love. However, we need to ask, "Does the Bible teach that?"

The writer of the New Testament book of Hebrews dealt with a similar question in his day. It goes almost without saying that the Hebrew nation had learned to trust in the one true God the hard way. God's instructions to the nation of Israel were crystal clear: "Hear, O Israel: The Lord our God, the Lord is one. Love the Lord your God with all your heart and with all your soul and with all your strength" (Deuteronomy 6:4–5 NIV).

Under Joshua's leadership, the Israelites conquered the Promised Land. Something strange happened after Joshua and his contemporaries died. "After that whole generation had been gathered to their ancestors, another generation grew up who knew neither the Lord nor what he had done for Israel. Then the Israelites did evil in the eyes of the Lord and served the Baals" (Joshua 2:10–11 NIV).

For the next eight hundred years or so, Israel's story was one of worshipping idols and false gods interspersed with years of devotion to the one true God. Idolatry ran rampant through the nation as they refused to serve the Living God. Their history settled the question. To our God, it matters that we serve and believe in only him. The prophets warned the nation that they must serve only the Lord God. When they failed to heed the warnings, catastrophes fell on them, everything from foreign invasions to natural disasters.

Still, they did not listen. God loved them so much, He warned them so often until finally he sent them into captivity to the Babylonian empire for seventy years. It was during this time the nation repented of their idolatry and never again served false gods.

In the book of Hebrews, a new religion is on the scene—Christianity. Many had accepted Jesus as the fulfillment of the Old Testament prophecies, which promised the Messiah would take away their sins. Then, as now, the problem was sin and Christ is the answer. Many of these new believers were tempted to give up on Christ and go back to the old Jewish ways. But they were warned that there is only one way to deal with the sin issue: Jesus Christ!

The w hole theme of Hebrews can be wrapped up in three words: Christ is greater.

Chapters 1–2: He is greater than the Angels. "In the past God spoke to our ancestors through the prophets at many times and in various ways, but in these last days he has spoken to us by his Son, whom he appointed heir of all things, and through whom also he made the universe. The Son is the radiance of God's glory and the exact representation of his being, sustaining all things by his powerful word. After he had provided purification for sins, he sat down at the right hand of the Majesty in heaven. So he became as much superior to the angels as the name he has inherited is superior to theirs" (1:1–4 NIV).

Chapters 3–4: He is greater than Moses. "Jesus has been found worthy of greater honor than Moses, just as the builder of a house has greater honor than the house itself" (3:3 NIV). Moses was considered a great prophet who gave them the Law of God.

Chapters 5–7: He is Greater than the priests. The high priests had to offer up annual sacrifices for his own sins and then for the sins of the people. To make Christ a greater high priest, his Father established him in a greater priesthood. "Son though he was, he learned obedience from what he suffered and, once made perfect, he became the source of eternal salvation for all who obey him and was designated by God to be high priest in the order of Melchizedek" (5:8–10 NIV).

Take a glimpse at just how much greater he is as a high priest! "Now there have been many of those priests, since death prevented them from continuing in office; but because Jesus lives forever, he has a permanent priesthood. Therefore he is able to save completely those who come to God through him, because he always lives to intercede for them" (7:23–25 NIV).

Chapters 8–10: Not to belabor the point, but Christ established a greater new covenant, in a greater heavenly worship center (tabernacle or temple), with a greater sacrifice for sin (his own blood). "But when Christ came as high priest of the good things that are now already here, he went through the greater and more perfect tabernacle that is not made with human hands, that is to say, is not a part of this creation. He did not enter by means of the blood of goats and calves; but he entered the Most Holy Place once for all by his own blood, thus obtaining eternal redemption" (9:11–12 NIV).

You see, it really does matter what we believe. The Old Testament ruled out all other religions that do not worship the Lord God. The New Testament reveals that all the laws of the old are fulfilled in the new through Jesus Christ. It is this very same Jesus who declared, "I am the way and the truth and the life. No one comes to the Father except through me" (John 14:6 NIV.

This all sounds pretty absolute to me.

ABOUT THE AUTHOR

Author Charles Lemaster writes from the perspective of someone who has been there. In his folksy writing style, he illuminates Bible truth from the viewpoint of personal transparency. He is an alumnus of Cedarville University, Ohio, and a graduate of Appalachian Bible College, West Virginia.

He served as a pastor and conference speaker for fourteen years in Ohio and Western New York State. Most recently he leads the "Hope Sunday School Class" in his home church as well as small group Bible studies. He regularly conducts worship at a local retirement, assisted living center in Miamisburg, Ohio and periodically preaches in his home church.

Diagnosed with Bipolar Disorder, he has spent the last almost 20 years learning how to manage his mental illness from a biblical perspective. He describes himself as "one beggar showing other beggars where to find bread." His burden and desire is to help encourage other folks with bipolar disorder and their families to live a blessed life through their commitment to Christ.

He and his wife, Pam, reside in West Carrollton, Ohio.

Lightning Source UK Ltd.
Milton Keynes UK
UKHW010752110821
388656UK00001B/83

9 781956 074499